Western Images, Western Landscapes

Western Images,

Western Landscapes

TRAVELS ALONG U.S. 89

Thomas R. Vale

Geraldine R. Vale

THE UNIVERSITY OF ARIZONA PRESS

TUCSON

The University of Arizona Press
Copyright © 1989
The Arizona Board of Regents
All Rights Reserved

93   92   91   90   89   5   4   3   2   1

LIBRARY OF CONGRESS CATALOGING-IN-PUBLICATION DATA
Vale, Thomas R., 1943–
    Western images, western landscapes : travels along u.s. 89/
Thomas R. Vale, Geraldine R. Vale.
        p.   cm.
    Bibliography: p.
    Includes index.
    ISBN 0-8165-1117-9
    1. West (U.S.)—Description and travel—1981–   2. Landscape—
West (U.S.) 3. United States Highway 89. 4. West (U.S.)—Geography.
5. Vale, Thomas R., 1943–   —Journeys—West (U.S.) 6. Vale, Geral-
dine R.—Journeys—West (U.S.)   I. Vale, Geraldine R.
II. Title.
F595.3.V35 1989
917.804'33—dc20   89-5063
                                                             CIP

British Library Cataloguing in Publication data are available.

FOR JIM PARSONS AND DAN LUTEN, *fellow geographers who showed us that curiosity about landscapes goes hand in hand with love of landscapes*

Contents

Illustrations

We are grateful to the people of the National Geographic Society, whose grant number 2668-83 supported a summer of fieldwork for this project. We appreciate the work of the University of Wisconsin Cartography Lab, particularly Associate Director Onno Brouwer and staff cartographer Kathryn Chapin, who prepared the maps.

The West:
An Introduction

The western United States, the American West, or, simply, the West, is a region whose name evokes a myriad of mental images. It is a landscape of mountains and deserts, of cattle ranches and wilderness areas, of sprawling suburban cities and languishing ghost towns. It is a land for exploding atomic bombs and spending summer vacations, for irrigated agriculture, oil exploration, and golden-age retirement. The West is a place for individuals to pursue the American dream and for the country's people to seek their collective future.

Such perceptions resonate with the western landscape. The mental images influence how humans treat the West and thus help determine the appearance of the western scene. But the physical landscape also helps to determine the mental images, by reinforcing or modifying what is in the mind. Our book is an exploration of this resonance, this interplay between mental image and landscape image in the American West.

Our effort is not intended to be a travel guide to a particular highway or to a particular area, although it might be used in those ways. Rather, it is an exploration of a geographical region, the American West, and what that region means to people. It has been written by two geographers who grew up in the West, who love the West, and who, although now living in Wisconsin, will always consider home to be the West.

"Set off primarily by the punctuation-points created by two great cities, the 636-mile stretch of U.S. 40 between Kansas City and Denver possesses also some geographical and topographical unity. At Kansas City the highway leaves not only the state of Missouri but also, approximately speaking, the rolling and wooded lands. Ahead, all the way to Denver, stretches the open country. . . . On the right kind of day—and there are many of them—you can watch the great white clouds piling up, and massing, and ever-changing. Then you inhale the great openness of the country and feel the spirit expand, and—as you keep your foot well down on the throttle— you can see, hour by hour, the East gradually shifting over to be the West."

GEORGE R. STEWART
U.S. 40

"When Bruce drove west in June . . . he drove directly from rainy spring into deep summer, from prison into freedom. . . . He was a westerner, whatever that was. The moment he crossed the Big Sioux and got into the brown country where the raw earth showed, the minute the grass got sparser and air dryer and the service stations less grandiose and the towns rattier, the moment he saw his first lonesome shack on the baking flats with a tipsy windmill creaking away at the reluctant underground water, he knew approximately where he belonged. . . . At sunset he was still wheeling across the plains toward Chamberlain, the sun fiery through the dust and the wide wings of the west going red to saffron to green as he watched, and the horizon ahead of him vast and empty and beckoning like an open gate. At ten o'clock he was still driving, and at twelve. As long as the road ran west he didn't want to stop, because that was where he was going, west beyond the Dakotas toward home."

WALLACE STEGNER
Big Rock Candy Mountain

CONCEPTS

Landscape Meanings

LANDSCAPE INTERPRETATION

The prehistoric Californian, rising early to search for black-tailed deer in the hills of the Coast Range to the west and observing a thick mist rolling through a mountain pass and tumbling into the interior valley of his home, probably wondered about the cause and effect: What god had sent this, and why? Was this a sign of good hunting, or an omen of evil? Today's suburbanite, maneuvering his Honda Civic into the early morning westward flow of commuter traffic and glancing up to a similar scene, may also wonder about the cause—Is this fog, smoke, or smog? And the effect—Will it cool down the valley heat, waft the flames of a grass fire toward his new condo, or fill his lungs with carcinogens?

The emotions generated by these questions and the attitudes resulting after a quest for the answers would be affected by the general outlook of both the viewer's culture and the viewer as an individual, as well as by some objective truth, however elusive or deceptive. The Pleistocene man whose societal group respected an evil Shroud Spirit may have felt apprehension and fear, but one who worshiped a benevolent Mist Maiden may have experienced pleasurable anticipation and delight. The mid-twentieth-century homeowner forewarned of the fire danger in the dry, steep-walled side canyons of the valley, or the contemporary environmentalist who has been inundated with literature bewailing the rampant ill effects of chemicals on human, beast, and plant might be anxious and dismayed. On the other hand, the suburbanite photographer who slips off the freeway at the cloverleaf to spread the legs of his tripod and capture the unusual form and light of the mist and haze, despite their cause or effect on temperature, real estate, or air quality, may feel awe and admiration. For millennia, then, clouds and haze have appeared in the Coast Range with daily and seasonal regularities, but the meanings associated with those landscape features have probably varied from society to society, group to group, and, even, individual to individual.

In spite of the common-sense recognition of multiple reactions to landscapes and landscape features, such as fog, some observers have attempted to identify a single dominant reaction, a single truth, held by most individuals in a society, or even by most individuals generally. David Lowenthal (1968), for example, has characterized the American perception of the American landscape as if the individuals and groups in American society were one homogeneous, monolithic mass. He suggests that "the classic reaction to [the immensity of] American space is that of [author O. E.] Rolvaag's pioneer wife, Beret, who dreaded the 'endless plain'"; also, he claims that in America "the virtual absence of man's artifacts appalled [and appalls] viewers." Inquiry into American landscape tastes would reveal these sentiments, but even cursory reading would also reveal admiration for the vastness and wildness of the continent. Consider Wallace Stegner's (1963) appreciation of the "endless plain": "The drama of this landscape is in the sky, pouring with light and always moving. . . . The beauty I am struck by . . . is a fusion: this sky would not be so spectacular without this earth to change and glow and darken under it. . . . Desolate? Forbidding? There was never a country that in its good moments was more beautiful." Or, reflect on Willa Cather's (1927) echoing of an American sentiment when her character Father Latour articulated his affection for the landscapes that had a "virtual absence of man's artifacts" in the wildness of New Mexico: "Beautiful surroundings, the society of learned men, the charm of noble women, the graces of art, could not make up to him the loss of those light-hearted mornings of the desert. . . . He had noticed that this peculiar quality of the air of new countries vanished after they were tamed by man. . . . He did not know just when it had become so necessary to him. . . . Something wild and free, something that whispered to the ear on the pillow, lightened the heart, softly, softly picked the lock, slid the bolts, and released the prisoned spirit of man into the wind, into the blue and gold, into the morning, into the morning!"

"Whom shall we quote?" Yi-Fu Tuan (1971) has asked rhetorically in recognizing the ambiguity and diversity of feelings toward landscape. "He who knows the truth," one might answer, but the simplicity inherent in such an answer is pointed out by Daniel Luten (1966): "If you seek patterns of consistency in such attitudes [toward landscapes], you had better start off with a far more durable lantern than Diogenes possessed." We see, nevertheless,

LANDSCAPE MEANINGS. Landscapes take on meanings only as reflections of human values. (Drawing by Koren; copyright © 1979 The *New Yorker Magazine,* Inc.)

at least one noteworthy pattern in the above examples: In contrast to immigrants or foreigners, native-born Americans are more likely to find their homeland appealing than appalling. Europe was the homeland of O. E. Rolvaag, as well as of his character, Beret, and it is the adopted home of Lowenthal; both Stegner and Cather, on the other hand, not only were born in America but also spent most of their childhood in treeless plains much like those Beret feared.

The interpretation of landscape as desirable or undesirable, however, is based upon more than length of residency. Donald Meinig (1979) has identified at least ten major "organizing ideas" by which people assign meaning to the visual scene, and from these meanings come the assessments of value, of good and bad. For example, the immense size of wheat farms on the Great Plains may be seen as "good" by the Plains farmers who have long appreciated the economic necessity for large-scale agriculture in these semi-arid acreages of relatively low productivity; for such viewers, the organizing idea may be one of "aesthetics" or "habitat." For someone else, knowledgeable about the potential effects of plowing in this landscape, the vast but relatively widely spaced rows of wheat may portend another disastrous dust bowl and appear as a "problem" created by human endeavor. Still other viewers might see the expanse of fields through the eyes of "ideology"—America is rich and productive; to them, the farmland is symbolic of American strength and greatness.

Similar to the cultivated grain fields of the Plains, the wildness of the Rocky Mountains may be viewed in favorable or negative terms according to the viewer's main organizing idea. Viewed as habitat by an inveterate devotee of the urban or agricultural scene, these stretches may be less than inviting, for they lack the human artifacts which are part of the most desired of landscapes, a harmonious blending of nature and culture. However, that same wildness would be viewed with pleasurable nostalgia as the precursor to modern civilization by those with a heightened sense of American history, and as a veritable utopia by those whose ideal is unadulterated nature.

This recognition of the variety in feelings toward and interpretations of landscape is not, then, meant to suggest that such reactions are without bounds or patterns. Rather, the diversity itself might be part of the organized generalization. Somewhere between the monolithic characterization of an entire society and the chaotic variability of individual differences are generalizations about landscape meanings that represent the values of large or otherwise significant segments of a human society.

REGIONAL LANDSCAPE MEANINGS

An individual landscape which is seen as typical of a larger region may evoke images and emotions which reflect a person's feelings about the region in general. The bank of ocean fog rolling over the coastal hills and through the Golden Gate may suggest to many the vibrant but eccentric society of the West Coast; a flat expanse of rectangular wheat fields stretching to an endless horizon may elicit a sense of solid, wholesome, conservative mid-America; a whitewashed mansion fronted by a porch of tall pillars and bordered by sprawling, lichen-draped oaks may suggest to a viewer the antebellum South, a refined society "gone with the wind." These interpretations of typically regional landscapes, moreover, may vary from person to person. The southern mansion, for example, may suggest a brutal and racist community, or an agricultural system that exploited the soil, or a land of farmers tied close to the land, in addition to the society of refinement. One typically regional landscape, then, may evoke a whole series of related images that reflect individual preconceptions of that region and individual attitudes toward what it represents.

THE AMERICAN WEST—IMAGES IN THE MIND

In what ways do people think about the American West? What are the mental images that people have about the region? Several natural characteristics come quickly to mind. The West is mountainous, justifying for many its description as "the handsome half of the continent." The West's gray and tan and brown tones reveal its aridity and prompt dismay from visitors accustomed to the verdure of the humid East. The West is environmentally diverse, reflecting the ruggedness of its topography and the steepness of its climatic gradients. Clearly true, these natural features, however, are incomplete expressions of landscape meanings. Like the fog blowing across California's coastal hills, such meanings depend upon human involvement with and valuation of place.

Both scholarly and popular writers have tried to identify the West's characteristics as a region for humans and to articulate its economic, social, and cultural relationship to the rest of the country (DeVoto 1934; Webb, W. P. 1936; Smith 1950; Morgan, N. 1961; Hollon 1966; Savage 1975; Gressley 1977; Bergon and Papanikolas 1978; Garreau 1981; Popper 1984); many have even attempted to expose misconceptions of those characteristics (Stegner 1971; Goetzmann 1981; Pyne 1981; McGrath 1984). Still, the simplicity of the single image is appealing; several recent books portray the West in terms of particular characterizations. For example, Rob Schultheis' (1983) *The Hidden West: Journeys in the American Outback* explores the West as an existing, sparsely settled frontier. William Allard's (1982) *Vanishing Breed: Photographs of the Cowboy and the West* presents the West's frontier as a phenomenon of past history. Lamm and McCarthy's (1982) *The Angry West* looks at the West as the source of wealth for other parts of the country. Satterfield and Muench's (1978) *Lewis and Clark Country* lauds the beauty of the West's wild lands.

As a preliminary step in our research for this book, we identified from the voluminous studies of the West eight mental images as encompassing the major characteriza-

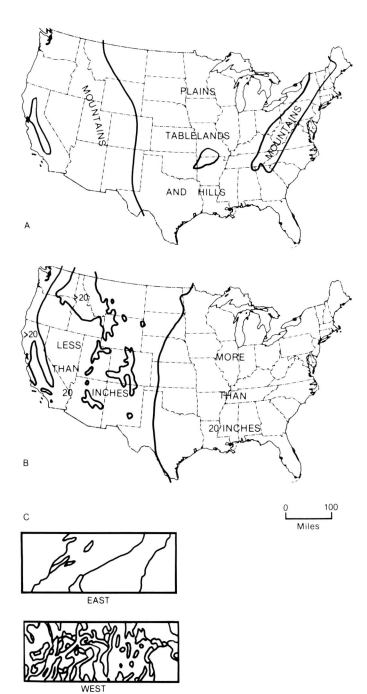

NATURAL FEATURES OF THE WEST.
Several natural characteristics of the
American West are distinctive: (a) the
West is mountainous; (b) the West is
dry, with only the Pacific Northwest
and high mountain oases receiving
more than twenty inches of precipitation annually; (c) the West is biologi-
cally and environmentally diverse, as
suggested by the much finer pattern-
ing of vegetation in an area of Utah
and Nevada than in a comparably
sized area of Tennessee, Virginia, and
Kentucky. (Maps adapted from *National Atlas of the United States*)

A westerner's view of an easterner's view of the United States.

WEST AS WASTELAND. Empty and arid regions of the Interior West are often viewed as wasteland, unimportant except as land that might provide security for the rest of the country. The West as Wasteland is but one vision of the region as a land to be exploited, as an Empty Quarter. (Cartoon: OLIPHANT copyright © 1981 UNIVERSAL PRESS SYNDICATE.

tions of the region that emphasize people-land interactions. They are described below, and they are ordered to emphasize their relationship to the historical development of the American West by European civilization. They are not mutually exclusive; many overlap. Some are similar to one another but vary in emphasis or perspective. Some contradict each other; others are more compatible.

1. *Empty Quarter.* The first explorers from Europe often viewed North America as land to be plundered of its riches. So, too, is the West often seen as a colony of the rest of the country. For example, Joel Garreau (1981), borrowing an English translation of an Arabic phrase used by the imperial British, likened the coal-rich northern Interior West to the oil-rich Middle East; according to Garreau, the region is "being chewed up and spit out in order to light our lamps and power our air conditioners." A key to this image is the view of the Interior West as too sparsely settled and too weak politically to defend its interests against forces from outside. It represents a continuation of a world view that extends far back in time.

2. *Frontier.* This is the West as the "Wild West," the "Cowboy West," the "Old West." It is the West of a "new continent" on which civilization has made only a token appearance. In the past, its characters were the Indians, fur-trappers, trail blazers, outlaws, cowboys. Today, the

Native Americans and cowboys are the remaining players, and the acts are staged in a setting of open rangelands and herds of range cattle, false-front buildings, and wide, wooden sidewalks, as well as a few bison and pronghorn, remnants of the nearly natural continent now lost everywhere in America but in the West. It was this image for which Robert Redford (1976) searched in a part of Utah: "The Outlaw Trail. It was a name that fascinated me—a geographical anchor in Western folklore. . . . I had been told the trail was real, that you could find parts still in existence, if you knew where to look."

3. *Big Rock Candy Mountain.* This is the West as a land of unbounded opportunity, a land for amassing personal wealth, a land for the good life, a land in which to achieve the American dream. Its symbols are those of wealth—natural wealth like untapped resources of minerals or timber, or, in the contemporary landscape, urban wealth symbolized by sprawling, booming suburban cities. It is an image that has influenced generations of Americans who, like Wallace Stegner's (1943) fictitious Bo Mason, were drawn "over the next range on the Big Rock Candy Mountain, that place of impossible loveliness that had pulled the whole nation westward, the place where the fat land sweated up wealth and heavens dropped lemonade."

4. *Middle Landscape.* Wilbur Zelinsky (1973) suggests that "the almost intuitive westering urge of the American migrant . . . cannot be fully explained as the search for economic advantage. . . . We may be witnessing the pursuit of an ever-receding mythic landscape, a pastoral perfection that has always lain to the westward, first for the European, and later for the American." The usual landscape of this "pastoral perfection" is a homogenized blending of the natural and the cultural into fields, pastures, farmhouses, and villages, much like the print on a traditional Christmas card featuring a rural scene in New England. In much of the American West, however, the combination of nature and culture takes a distinctive form: Wild nature and civilized culture remain distinct but in close juxtaposition to one another—a field of hay against a red rock slope, a cluster of homes on a desert plain, a small town in a mountain valley. Such landscapes suggest a stability of opposing forces in a balance, a harmony, a garden, a Middle Landscape.

5. *Turnerian Progression.* Continued growth and development may destroy the "pastoral perfection" and create a landscape in which humans seem to dominate over nature—the city. The urban scene as an endpoint in uni-

directional change reflects the scheme of Frederick Jackson Turner (1894): "The record ... begins with the Indian and the hunter. ... It goes on to tell of ... the trader ... the pastoral stage in ranch life, the exploitation of the soil ... in sparsely settled communities; [it continues with] the intensive culture of the denser farm settlement; and finally the manufacturing organization with city and factory system." The wilderness, the frontier, the farming town are merely predictable, temporary stages of an inevitable progression. In such terms, large western cities are seen as the culminating end-point of the process.

6. *Desert.* In the West, the farms prosper and cities grow according to the local availability of water. The lack of abundant water, some argue, is a characteristic that gives the West unity and uniqueness. Dryness influences the natural landscape, but it also affects human use of the land, as Walter Prescott Webb (1936) argued. John Wesley Powell (1878) recognized the constraints that aridity imposed on western settlement and western land policy a century ago. "The very condition of aridity from which Powell's warning stemmed makes the consequences of mismanagement catastrophic. ... What ruins a farm family may also ruin the land, and hence all future farmers in that place" (Stegner 1962a). This vision sees the arid rangelands as overgrazed, the shallow soils as salinized, the delicate valley bottoms as gullied, the warm air as smog-filled. It is a West of aridity, and because of that aridity, it is a land of vulnerable human endeavors and ruined natural features. It is a West as Desert.

7. *Protected Wild Nature.* With the rise of modern, urbanized, American society, the West has increasingly assumed two additional roles, and thus two additional images. The first focuses on the West's function as protected wild landscape, and the value placed on wild nature that reserves such as national parks and wilderness areas represent. The development of this concern for wild nature reflects, according to Daniel Luten (1969), the transformation of the United States population from poor to rich. As early colonial society, whose members struggled to subdue nature for their survival, evolved to concerned, prosperous American citizens with enough leisure time to assess the changing landscape, there developed "the proposition that the landscape should be saved because it is beautiful." The West contains the bulk of such protected lands, and this regional identity reflects the area's link to the rest of the nation, a nation sufficiently rich to value wild nature as a resource.

8. *Playground.* People travel to national parks not only
to observe wild nature but also to enjoy outdoor recreation, and they travel to the American West for the outdoor
recreation offered not only in the parks but also in a myriad of attractions both contemporary and historical, in-
doors and outdoors, public and private. This travel suggests the second of the more recently acquired images of
the West, a Playground. The trip for winter skiing, the
outing to pursue big game or mountain trout, the wanderings for sightseeing, and especially the time for the two-
week, family vacation in summer—each focuses on the
American West. With his 1985 country hit song, B. J.
Thomas epitomizes this popular culture image of the Interior West: "If we don't get to Paris, it won't break our
hearts; we'll just pack up the kids and go to Yellowstone
Park."

THE AMERICAN WEST—IMAGES ON THE LAND

These eight images have been explored by authors who
have used as data and evidence primarily the written and
oral record of the West. To what degree, we wondered, are
these mental images manifested in the landscapes of the
American West? In order to make this assessment, a
sample of western landscapes, images on the land, was
needed. Where should one search for these landscapes that
typify the American West?

Although not focusing on landscape meanings, the authors of the various articles and books about the American West often have used photographs and paintings to
supplement their texts, recognizing that landscape interpretation is a fundamental way by which individuals and
society form or reinforce impressions of a region. Often,
these scenes are from the Interior West, which extends
from the High Plains to the Sierra Nevada-Cascade mountains. So defined, the "typical" American West specifically excludes the Pacific slope of California, Oregon, and
Washington; although this area shares many characteristics with the Interior West, it has others, such as heavier
precipitation, greater urbanization, and a stronger concern
for environmental issues, that set it apart (Vance 1972;
Garreau 1981). Just as this identification of the Pacific
slope as distinct from the American West generally is not
capricious, neither is it recent. Even John Gunther in his
1947 classic book, *Inside U.S.A.*, made this very point:
"California, Oregon, and Washington are not 'the West' at
all. . . . People on the Pacific Coast think of themselves as
belonging to the 'coast'; the 'West' is quite something else

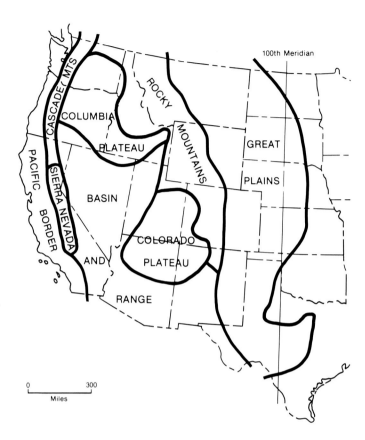

PHYSIOGRAPHIC REGIONS. The Interior West, the heart of the American West, extends from the Great Plains westward to the Sierra Nevada-Cascade Mountains.

again. . . . Normally, when saying 'West' with any discrimination, we mean the eight [mountain] states—Montana, Idaho, Nevada, Utah, Colorado, Wyoming, New Mexico, and Arizona. . . . In Portland I actually heard a lady say that she was 'going West' on a brief trip—and she meant Utah!" (Gunther 1947).

THE AMERICAN WEST—THIS STUDY

As typically western scenes, then, we selected landscapes along a cross section of the Interior West, the route of U.S. Highway 89 from Nogales, Arizona, to near St. Mary, Montana. This route provides a cross-section of the Interior West not only in space but also in terms of the landscape characteristics through which or beside which it passes—natural environments, natural resources, land uses, economic activities, densities of settlements, human histories; simply stated, U.S. 89 samples the landscapes of the Interior West. We traveled this highway on three trips between 1982 and 1984 (and parts of the route on innumerable other trips over the last two decades),

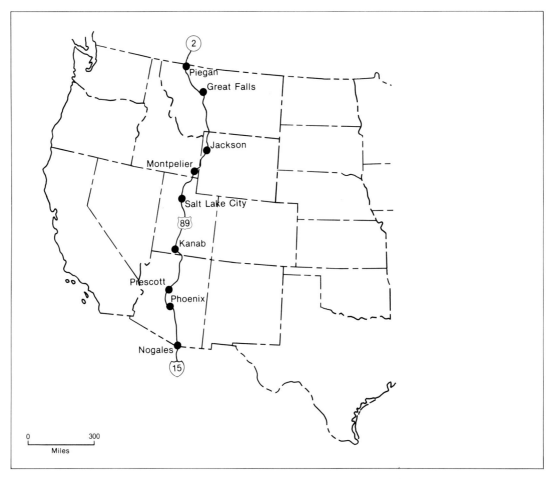

U.S. HIGHWAY 89

concentrating our senses on the observable scene and trying to document by pen and by shutter the raw material as it presented itself and to analyze how it conformed to or deviated from the eight images. We wrote about and photographed common landscapes that we felt were representative of what existed along the route. Views that were particularly scenic or blighted were not specifically sought, although they also were not necessarily avoided. We did not select views that provided artistic, abstract patterns, nor did we search for portraits of interesting, local people. We seldom focused on close, intimate views of features, but, rather, we stressed a scale that approximates what an auto traveler might see from a car window. If people seem absent from our photographs, it is partly because humans are not as conspicuous in typical landscapes, especially in the Interior West, as one might think; on several occasions, we consciously *tried* to include people in photographs, even if that inclusion seemed to stress humans more than landscape. But the absence of still more people in our photographs is consistent with our purpose: Our general goal was to portray *landscapes* that seemed typical of the visual scene.

The use of landscapes so sampled and photographed deserves some further discussion. An analogy to painting is appropriate. Heller and Williams (1982), in their book *Painters of the American Scene*, identify two main approaches to landscape painting. The first school is that of the "romantics," artists who are "less interested in capturing the physical appearance of a place than in using the image of landscape to evoke a mood or to reveal [their] inner feelings." Most landscape portrayals in photography, painting, and literature seem to belong to this school, expressing in the particular medium what the artist already feels about a region. In other words, artists often manipulate the landscape scenes so that the resulting portrayal elucidates or intensifies for the viewer or reader their own preconceived emotion, attitude, or belief. Heller and Williams identify the other school as "regionalists," artists who are primarily interested "in capturing and defining the character of each of the country's regions" by recording "the scene's topography rather than exploiting its dramatic potential." Compared to the first school, this second approach is more akin to the search for and identification of order—in this case in the character of regions—that is an essence of science. We were more closely aligned to this latter school as we made our journey from border to border. We tried to work from the unaltered, unmanipulated scenes to read what the common landscape seems to say to an interested observer. Our question, then, was not how we could manipulate the landscape to dramatize our attitudes toward the region, but rather how we could capture and define the unaltered landscape and determine how it manipulates the viewer's mind to create a particular sense of place.

We are attempting to approach the landscape as scientists, albeit qualitative scientists, rather than as artists. Our purpose is a quest for knowledge, an inquiry, rather than an attempt to get a preconceived message across to an audience. This is not a photographic study of an area in the usual artistic sense, but a scientific study using both personal observation and photography to collect information before analyzing it. Moreover, and also akin to more conventional "science," we are interested in generalization: What features or characteristics in the visual scene are essential parts of "western" landscapes? The fieldwork resulted in copious notes and hundreds of photographs, both in color and black and white. The reader is presented with our analysis and conclusions as well as what we have determined to be representative data. Fifty-two of the original photographs supplement the text.

We approached the interpretation of these recorded landscapes by asking an initial question: What evidence might a viewer see that would suggest or contradict any of the mental images? In attempting to answer this question, we encountered related questions. In formulating our answers, we depended primarily upon the features and images that the landscape presented, but supplemented them with information from magazines, journals, newspapers, books, and personal conversations.

Can this attempt at landscape interpretation succeed? For an answer, let us begin our northbound trip on U.S. 89 on the Mexico-United States border in Nogales, Arizona.

TRAVELS ALONG U.S. 89

Nogales to Phoenix

U.S. 89 begins at the international border station in Nogales, Arizona, named for its bucolic location in the Los Nogales (Spanish for walnuts) Valley but developed as a railroad town because of its stategic position near Nogales Pass. The highway in the United States represents a continuation of Mexican federal route 15, up from Hermosillo, and on a grander scale, of the Pan American highway from Central America. For 3000 miles northward, U.S. 89 passes through landscapes of gentle plains and rugged mountains, sunny desert and dark forest, quiet towns and bustling cities, green pastures and golden fields of wheat—a fine representative cross-section of the western United States of America. But here, for the first time in December of 1982, we found so many contradistinctions to those more common Western scenes as almost to suggest that we were somewhat south, rather than a short distance north, of the international border. Our confusion did not stem only from the vegetation, too rich in grass and trees to fit the usual image of the arid southwestern United States. Nor was it so much that Spanish seemed more common than English on the bold advertisements that adorned the storefronts, or that dark-complected shoppers easily outnumbered those fairer-skinned tourists like us, from the Upper Midwest, on the sidewalks and in the shops below. Nor was it simply that our gaze southward brought a view of much-less-than-modest homes, without freshly painted walls, without manicured yards, without, even, paved streets. It was all of those things, we suppose, and others that we cannot articulate.

But certainly one experience, in a cherished American institution, drove home to us our location at the edge of our country. The McDonald's restaurant near the border station offered a complete menu in Spanish and a gallon-size jar of jalapeño peppers with a set of tongs so that customers could pile as many as they wanted onto their "Gran Mac" sandwiches. While we waited in line for nearly ten minutes, the only English we heard was that of our own conversation. If we had wished, we even could have traded in our change for pesos—at 135 to the dollar.

The intermingling of Mexican and American in Nogales reflects the nature of the international border—more
like a sieve than a barrier, with people and products moving in both directions. The newspapers were full of stories
of the absence of staple foods and materials in Mexico,
and our observations seemed to illustrate that fact. Citizens from south of the border flocked into the strategic-
ally located Safeway grocery and other nearby merchandise stores and emerged carrying large paper bags from
which typically protruded several loaves of bread and,
oddly, bundles of coat hangers. Some early morning arriv-
als even rummaged through the waste bins behind the
clothing stores, successfully beating the garbage trucks.
Citizens from the north seemed equally interested in the
stores of Mexico, whether for shirts or trinkets. Cars and
trucks passed with similar ease back and forth, although
vans and autos with trailers going into Mexico were receiving much more thorough attention than similar vehicles moving north; one late-model van was searched by
border guards who meticulously removed both the car-
peted internal paneling and the insulation in the walls of
the vehicle while the family looked on with apparent
calmness.

The contrast between Mexico and the United States is
emphasized, perhaps symbolized, by the tall and substantial, chain-link border fence. It stands as a conscious attempt to keep those without wealth from reaching the
"promised land," the land of the "good life." The number
of illegal aliens that cross the Mexican border (mostly into
Texas and California, rather than here into Arizona) is difficult to determine, but recent estimates suggest that
about two million "undocumented persons" are living in
the United States. Moreover, this total may be again increasing, in spite of the 1986 "amnesty" for undocumented resident aliens and stiffened penalties for hiring
illegal immigrants. Radicals argue that such migration reflects the fundamental inequality in wealth between the
two countries, and thus the human movement cannot be
eliminated without elimination of its cause. Liberals
point out that the resulting work force in the United
States is exploited because the aliens receive low pay and
no social benefits; they may not pay income taxes, but
they do pay sales taxes. According to their viewpoint, the
biggest beneficiaries of this system are the employers.
Conservatives contend that the jobs reduce opportunities
for workers who are United States citizens, particularly
the unskilled and unemployed. Whatever one's political

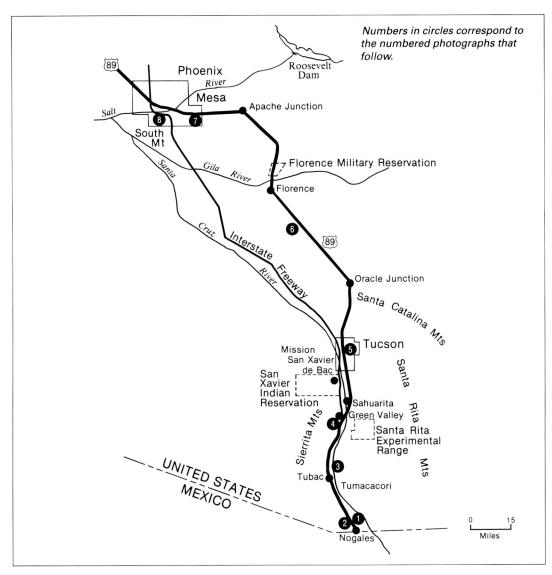

Numbers in circles correspond to the numbered photographs that follow.

NOGALES TO PHOENIX

stance, two points about illegal immigration are clear: First, with declining domestic fertility, immigration, whether legal or not, looms ever more important in the population growth of the country, and thus it inhibits the achievement of a stabilized population. Second, the desires of so many to cross into the southwestern states suggest the perpetuation of the American dream, the vision of a land of abundance and opportunity, the Big Rock Candy Mountain.

For almost four hundred miles north of Nogales, U.S. 89 crosses the basin and range country which characterizes the southern part of the Interior West. For its first seventy miles within this physiographic region, the highway follows the gentle valley of the Santa Cruz River, which originates in the mountains of Arizona before swinging south of the border and then northward to drop gradually in elevation from nearly 4,000 feet near Nogales to 2,400 feet in Tucson. Over those miles, the desert grassland around Nogales, rich in herbaceous plants and mesquite, is replaced by the Sonoran Desert vegetation of scattered low shrubs, stands of tall saguaro or short cholla cacti, and bare rocky soil. The distant mountains that line the route on either side for much of the way rise several thousand feet above the Santa Cruz and support grasslands, woodlands, and forests. Their relatively moist slopes and ravines feed the flow of the river which is lined by willows and cottonwoods, pastures and hayfields, cattle and horses.

As in many other such hospitable environments near the present-day international boundary, Spanish priests of the seventeenth century established missions along the Santa Cruz and spread the faith to the native populations. Spanish explorers also penetrated further into what would become Arizona in search of mineral wealth. (The New World generally and the American West specifically have been characterized for centuries as El Dorado, the land of gold.) The two purposes, God and gold, have been often intertwined, and this linkage is nowhere better illustrated than at Tumacacori, eighteen miles north of Nogales.

Founded on the site in about 1696 (the present building is much younger—it was dedicated in 1822), the mission at Tumacacori is one of three established by the Jesuits along the Santa Cruz River; the most famous of the three is San Xavier Del Bac near present-day Tucson. In 1767, King Carlos III of Spain ordered the expulsion of Jesuits from all of the Spanish empire—the king was apparently afraid of, perhaps with some justification, the growing power of the Jesuit order. Thus, in the midst of the sum-

1. Downtown Nogales, Arizona, southern end of U.S. 89. The houses on the hillslope at the extreme right are in Mexico.

2. Fence along international border in Nogales. Mexico is to the right of the fence and on the background slope.

mer heat, troops forced the missionaries, whether in Mexico City or in the remotest hinterlands such as Tumacacori, off the continent.

From this history were born the legends of buried treasures. Although the motivations for the establishment of the missions were conventionally religious, the myth-makers, skeptical of spiritual motives and confident of practical ones, convinced themselves that the real goal of the missions was the secret mining of gold and silver by Indian slaves for the benefit of the Church coffers. The hurried expulsion order, the reasoning continues, caught the Jesuits off-guard, and they were forced to leave their riches behind—buried in the floors or behind the walls of their missions, or sealed off in dynamited mine tunnels.

The mission at Tumacacori has been the focus for a particularly enduring fable of lost wealth. When Anglo miners searched the Santa Cruz River valley for gold and silver in the early nineteenth century, they were convinced that the old mission, abandoned since the middle of the previous century, had been the center of a successful mining operation. Vandalism on the mission grounds followed, and the search for the source of the still unfound riches took the ever-hopeful prospectors to the mountains south of Tumacacori. It is testimony to the optimism of the human spirit and the indefatigable belief in the Big Rock Candy Mountain that people still search abandoned missions and nearby mountain slopes for treasures that never were.

On our morning at Tumacacori, we searched for treasures other than gold or silver, immersing our twentieth century psyches in the rich history of the buildings occupied by European populations for nearly four hundred years. (What provincialism it is to suggest, as East Coast residents are wont to do, that the American West lacks a long human history and that, as a result, westerners cannot appreciate what it means to have a sense of involvement with particular places!) We also wandered about the mostly unkempt grounds of the national monument, catching a glimpse of a pyrrhuloxia, a grey-washed southern relative of the common all-red cardinal, in the treetops while trying to get a closer look at evasive birds fluttering among the mesquite, probably some species of wintering sparrow. As much as anything, we refugees from the Wisconsin winter enjoyed the mild, sunny December weather and the quiet, lonely peace of the place.

Other refugees, both seasonal and permanent, have been attracted to Arizona by the same sense of history and

3. Mission at Tumacacori. The grassy
vegetation with scattered mesquite,
here leafless in December, characterizes much of the hilly terrain of extreme southern Arizona.

BASIN AND RANGE. The Basin and
Range region of the Interior West is
characterized by mountain ranges
uplifted by faults and separated by
downfaulted basins. The most common alignment of these faults is
north-south or northwest-southeast,
and the resulting mountain ranges
have been thus described as "an army
of caterpillars crawling out of Mexico."
As much as the bare sandstone slick-
rock of southern Utah or the snow-
splotched ridges of Colorado, the Basin and Range topography symbolizes
the American West. (Figure adapted
from Hunt 1974)

recreation that we enjoyed at Tumacacori. We were struck by this fact increasingly as we drove along u.s. 89 north of the old mission.

Three miles north of Tumacacori lies one such attraction, the settlement of Tubac, established in 1752 by the Spanish as a military outpost for protection of settlers, missionaries, and Indian converts from hostile natives. The name Tubac (Pima for "where something rotted") derives from an Indian legend of an early battle and death, and during succeeding years Tubac continued to be besieged by Apaches as it was alternately occupied by a Mexican garrison, a Mormon community, and a silver-mining operation. Today, it is mostly a collection of arts and crafts galleries, a place where, as local promoters brag, "the arts and the West meet." The image of the Frontier is apparently desired, but perhaps a neater and cleaner frontier than that which formerly existed. Here, the old buildings are restored to look a little newer, the new buildings designed to appear much older. They house artists and potters, sculptors, and carvers. Browsing through them, we were attracted to one shop that offered cards and note paper attractively illustrated with plants and birds that are native not only to the deserts of Arizona but also, surprisingly, to the forests and prairies of the Upper Midwest. Questioned about this observation, the shopkeeper responded that the home and original shop of the artist were indeed in Michigan, but that the shop at Tubac reflected winter periods that the artist spent in central Arizona. In fact, she herself also was from Michigan, and she too enjoyed the mild weather of the Southwest in the cooler time of year. "But you have to get out of here before the heat of April and May—I stayed on in the shop one year until late May, and I thought that the heat would kill me on the drive back home." We were reminded of a similar conversation that we had overheard a few days earlier on the plane as it was descending to the Phoenix airport. A college-age girl who apparently lived in the desert below was describing the weather of her home to an attentive male sitting next to her. It is usually pleasantly warm in the winter, she said, but in summer it gets "really hot, up to 115 degrees." He thought that was too warm, and she hesitated before responding that it wasn't too bad "if you live near a pool—maybe in the pool." Like the shopkeeper, and like most of us, she seemed to embrace the Desert only with equivocation.

A second settlement, eighteen miles north of Tubac, illustrated more strongly the appeal of desert living, this

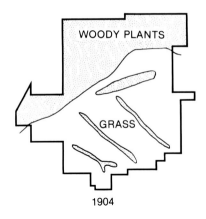

DESERT GRASSLAND. In the time before European colonization of North America, large areas of the semi-arid landscape of southern Arizona and New Mexico were covered by a grassland, usually called the desert grassland. Today, shrubs and small trees, notably mesquite, have increased greatly and have replaced much of the grass. Heavy grazing by Spanish livestock and the elimination of frequent burning probably contributed to this vegetation change, although a reduction in summer rainfall may also be a factor (Humphrey 1987). At the Santa Rita Experimental Range, a few miles southeast of Green Valley, the transformation has continued during this century and is documented in vegetation maps prepared by range ecologists. To the degree that the vegetation change reflects human use, and misuse, of the landscape, it exemplifies the vision of the Interior West as an abused arid environment, the Interior West as Desert. (Figure adapted from "Vegetation Changes on a Southern Arizona Grassland Range" by R. Humphrey and L. Mehrhoff, *Ecology* (1958), 39: 720–26. Copyright © 1958 by Ecological Society of America. Reprinted by permission)

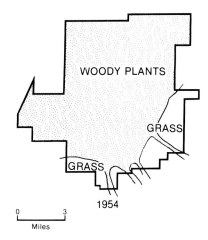

WOODY PLANTS

GRASS

GRASS

1954

0   3
Miles

4. Retirement community in Green Valley, Arizona. The modular homes have yards of gravel and desert plants, rather than lawns and shade trees. The Santa Rita Mountains, with a fringing pediment, rise in the distance.

time of a more permanent nature. Green Valley has been described as "the most attractive of Arizona's retirement communities." It sits on a gently sloping plain, a pediment, that rises to the west of the Santa Cruz River; the Santa Rita Mountains climb impressively to the southeast. In the sandy openings amid the mesquite, cacti of various sorts thrust their spiny stems and in spring their brilliant blossoms sunward, and thus the true desert seems more at hand than farther south.

Development at Green Valley began in 1963, and after initial fitful financial problems, the community of apartments, condominiums, and detached houses has grown impressively. Allegedly inspired by the Spanish Colonial architecture of the Mexican town of Alamos, near Guaymas, many of Green Valley's structures do seem to contain features that conform to the stereotypic image of southwestern buildings—single stories, adobe-like stuccos, arched walkways, walled patios, and wrought-iron window coverings. In one particularly appealing neighborhood, houses were set back from gently winding gravel roads, without borders of sidewalks or curbs but with dense plantings of cacti everywhere—in the yards, immediately beside the road pavement, and even in narrow strips separating traffic.

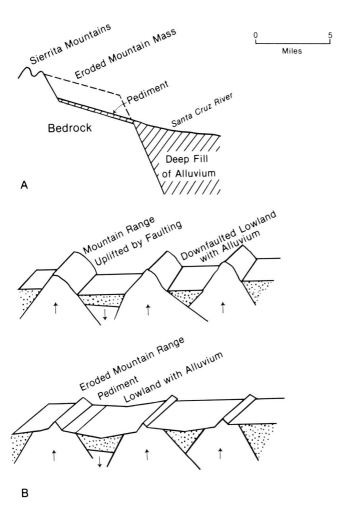

0 — 5
Miles

PEDIMENTS. The backward erosion of a mountain front generates a gently inclined bedrock surface called a pediment. The broad pediment at the base of the Sierrita Mountains has resulted from the retreat westward of the edge of the mountain mass. The rock debris eroded from the mountains has been carried by streams across the pediment into the lowest part of the basin where it has accumulated to great depths. This rock material deposited by streams is called alluvium. (Information for drawing of Sierrita Mountains pediment from Tuan 1959)

NORTHERN PART OF THE BASIN AND RANGE. Faulting remains strong and active here, and there has been little opportunity to erode back the mountain fronts to produce pediments. The lowland basins are simply deep accumulations of alluvium. In the south, by contrast, the mountain blocks have not been uplifted as much, and the long period of stability has allowed the backward erosion of the mountain fronts and the associated development of broad pediments. Some researchers believe that pediments may form in any climatic environment, and, in fact, interpret those of the American Southwest as relict features of a slightly more humid, but still semiarid, past, preserved in the more arid times of today. As no other landform, broad pediments suggest the long stability and dryness of the southern part of the Interior West.

Looking out over a clean and quiet residential area, with an open desert pediment beyond and the Santa Ritas in the far distance, we could believe that here, on a mild and sunny December day, with house finches singing and a covey of quail noisily foraging beneath a row of blooming oleander, we were in a sort of paradise. Green Valley is not the land of rich job opportunity that illegal aliens are seeking, nor is it the land of vast mineral treasures that the Spanish sought. The economic wealth of the retirement community, in fact, derives from without rather than from within. (Commercial activity is indeed quite limited here, and on one recent trip we even had difficulty locating the one motel in town, since the previously available adobe units—single and spacious—had apparently been converted to more permanent lodging.) What struck us as alluring about this scene was not its expression of material wealth, but rather the visual balance of nature and culture, neither dominating but both existing in an apparently harmonious blending of a Middle Landscape. Arizona seemed to be a land of promise and hope, of goodness, in more ways than one.

This Edenic impression of Arizona is shared by many people, a large number of whom act on their impressions and move to the Grand Canyon State. The popular concept of a massive "snow belt to sun belt" migration is only partly true, but Arizona's magnetism for migrants generally, and elderly migrants particularly, is strong. In an evaluation of internal migration within the United States, sociologist Jeanne Biggar (1979) found that Arizona is the only western state attracting large numbers of migrants from several "snow belt" states east of the Rockies—Michigan, Minnesota, Iowa, and Illinois. For the elderly, moreover, only three states in the "sun belt" seem to have particularly strong appeal, and those three states dominate as destinations for elderly migrants for the entire country—Arizona is one, along with California and Florida.

Why do people move to such states? For those who are earning an income, the image of available work is crucial, although it is not simply jobs that draw working people and certainly it is not jobs that entice the retired. Biggar invokes reasons that a person on the street might identify: "[It is] the general climate, the cost of living, and the lifestyle which have brought people to the Sunbelt. Climate takes on increasing importance as people have more time and money to enjoy leisure activities. The Sunbelt offers both more 'sun' and more 'fun.' Outdoor living, informal entertaining, and golf the year-round—all afford the new lifestyles which Americans have adopted." Maybe Green Valley is as much a Playground as a Middle Landscape.

Just north of Green Valley, u.s. 89 leaves Interstate 19 by swinging to the east, crosses the Santa Cruz River, and then again turns north toward Tucson. Immediately on the east side of the river, the highway enters a vast expanse of pecan orchards.

The orchard between Green Valley and Sahuarita is the world's largest area of cultivated pecans. About five thousand acres support nearly a quarter of a million trees. Planted in the late 1960s, this orchard marked the beginning of the pecan industry in Arizona, which has now spread to scattered locales from the southeast corner of the state to the Colorado River. Chosen for their low labor requirements and suitability for mechanization, pecans here replaced cotton fields at a time when the market for the fiber was weak. Although the country's production of pecans continues to be concentrated in the southeast, particularly Georgia, the few orchards of Arizona are much larger than their older and more numerous eastern predecessors.

The pecans typify a common image of Arizona, and western, agriculture—plantings of specialty crops. According to that image, the Garden of the Great Plains is covered by wheat, that of the Midwest by corn, and that of the South by soybeans and cotton, but the Garden of the West is home to grapes and oranges, avocados and artichokes, apricots and dates. While parts of the West are indeed the country's centers for such products, less glamorous crops are far more common. In Arizona, for example, nearly one half of the agricultural land is used to grow cotton, and one third supports alfalfa and grains. Only five percent is planted to vegetables and melons, and another five to citrus; pecans account for less than two percent of the state's agricultural land.

But the pecan orchards north of Green Valley do typify two characteristics of western agriculture. First, they are irrigated, demanding five to six acre-feet of water per acre per year. While this magnitude of water use is high even by western standards, the Desert of the American West requires irrigation water for most crops, whether in California, Idaho, or Arizona. Moreover, the amount of water used for irrigation easily dominates water use in the West; household, commercial, and industrial uses are proverbial drops in the bucket by comparison. In Arizona, ninety percent of the water consumed is for agriculture, and thus the groundwater pumping that is lowering water tables dramatically—here less than fifty feet but near Phoenix more than three hundred feet—is directly caused by agricultural water use. Of course, most of this water keeps alive alfalfa and cotton, rather than specialty crops like pecans. Critics of western water developments suggest, with reason, that water projects subsidized by public money help the agricultural industry more than the American diet.

And an industry it is. The pecan orchards are owned and operated by Farmer's Investment Company, or FICO. Such corporate management characterizes western agriculture generally and Arizona agriculture specifically. Since the beginning of western agriculture, the expense of water development has encouraged the domination of agriculture by companies rather than families.

The importance of big companies in the economy of Arizona is also represented by the immense tailings that rise west of the orchards, tailings of the Duval Corporation copper mine of the Pima Mining District. The extraction of copper in Arizona began after the development of the railroads in the latter part of the last century, but it has dominated the mining industry of the state in recent years, accounting for nearly two-thirds of all the copper mined in the country. It is an economic activity that provides jobs for workers and thus benefits the local population, although others have stressed that the major benefits, company profits, mostly leave not only the mining communities but also the state. Moreover, when economic considerations prompt closing of the mines, as has happened recently not only here in southern Arizona but also elsewhere in the Interior West, those who suffer the most are the local employees. These Empty Quarter images belie the sense of independence that the miners and their families often have of their livelihood.

We were aware of these interpretations of agriculture and mining on the days that we spent in the landscapes just north of Green Valley, but somehow they did not dominate our feelings about the place. We watched the harvesting of pecans with equipment that swept up the nuts, already mechanically shaken from the trees and raked into rows, until a patrolling security guard drew up alongside us and warned us away, however mildly, from entering the orchards. The entire scene suggested a Garden, although the mechanization and the need for security seemed violations of that image. We also found interesting, even amusing, the spindly and apparently sparsely irrigated ornamental trees planted in long rows atop the copper tailings. Could the Garden be reestablished on this artifact of an industrial society?

North of the pecan orchards and the mine tailings, and amid modest agricultural land with some commercial and residential development, the highway runs beside the deep gullying that characterizes the bottomlands of the Santa Cruz River Valley, gullying that is widespread in the American Southwest. Long a feature of geological and geographic interest, the causes of the stream downcutting in the region over the last century remain an unresolved question. Some scientists argue that changes in climate induced the gullying, but others see grazing by livestock, which denuded the slopes draining into the river and thereby increased runoff, as a crucial element. The recent national report on desertification in the United States em-

phasized the human abuse factor and pinpointed the
Santa Cruz River as a prime example of that abuse:

> Standing today atop the bank of the Santa Cruz River . . . it is
> almost impossible to imagine what this floodplain looked
> like a hundred years ago. Water flowed through an unchan-
> neled river that wound sluggishly across a flat, marshy area.
> Trout were abundant. Beavers built dams. There were giant
> cottonwood, mesquite, willow, sycamore, and paloverde, and
> grass—grass tall enough to 'brush a horse's belly', to shelter
> wild turkeys. Meandering, ungullied tributary creeks fed the
> river. Today the river channel is dry, a broad trench filled with
> nothing but gravel and sand. The River's bank is a bare dirt
> wall. . . . Mesquite clumps are so thick they are impassible.
> . . . The ground is bare. . . . Dry gullies—the River's tribu-
> taries—intersect the trench walls (Sheridan 1981).

Here is an unequivocal vision of the Southwest, of the Interior West, as a ruined arid land, as Desert.

After passing beside the San Xavier Indian Reservation
on the west and the Tucson airport on the east, u.s. 89, for
the next sixteen miles, is the major north-south business
route through the urban area of Tucson.

Long and wide, low in physical structure and population density, sprawling Tucson seems perplexing. It is the
oldest of the major settlements of Arizona, founded in
1775, a few months after the ride of Paul Revere on the
other side of the continent and another world away. At the
time, the Spanish wanted to move the presidio, formerly
at Tubac, closer to the Mission San Xavier del Bac and its
surrounding population of Spanish and Indian settlers;
they selected a spot that became Tucson. Isolation from
the outside world and threats from hostile Apaches, however, discouraged the town's growth for most of its existence. Only a little more than one hundred years ago and
not quite one hundred years after its beginning, Tucson
supported but a few hundred people; even at the turn of
the century its population was only 7500. Today, the city
has about 400,000 residents and a total urban population
of more than one-half million. On the one hand, Tucson
prides itself on its great age—Lawrence Clark Powell
(1976) reports that Tucsonians "patronize Phoenix even as
San Francisco scorns Los Angeles . . . . Was Tucson not the
Ancient and Honorable Old Pueblo?" Yet, city promoters
brag about the city as a "young, vibrant community," according to historian C. L. Sonnichsen (1982), and the location of its original reason for existence, its Spanish presidio, is now surrounded by a sprawling modern city. The
imagery of Tucson—a town of the Frontier, a Garden

5. Homes in a modest neighborhood near downtown Tucson.

settlement, or a manifestation of Turnerian growth?—is confused.

Much in Tucson fits the image of a sort of Nirvana, "a somewhat spiny and superheated corner of Paradise," as Sonnichsen (1982) suggests. Tucson's physical setting is impressive: The Santa Catalina Mountains rise to nearly 10,000 feet northeast of the city; the most luxuriant of Sonoran Desert vegetation stretches away in all directions; and the weather combines mild, dry winters with glorious summer clouds that adorn *Arizona Highways* magazine. Tourists find much that attracts them—the movie lots of Old Tucson, the animals of the Arizona-Sonora Desert Museum, the "finest of old Spanish missions" at San Xavier, the expanses of wild landscape in Saguaro National Monument, the craft shops of the old downtown, and the best Mexican food anywhere in the United States. Much of this mix of attractions reflects both the natural environment and the richness of Tucson's past and present culture, which involves Hispanics and Indians as well as Anglos.

New residents as well as tourists are drawn to Tucson, with net migration accounting for 3 percent of the city's 4 percent annual growth in the 1970s. Such in-migration seems justified; the popular *Places Rated Almanac* (Boyer and Savagean 1985) ranked Tucson as the seventy-ninth most desirable city of the 329 evaluated as places in which

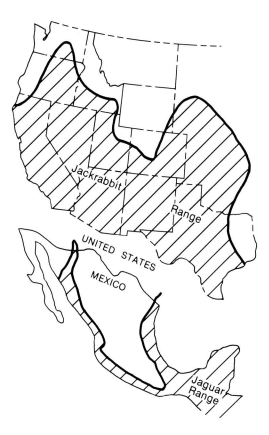

JACKRABBITS AND JAGUARS. An unexpected Nature characterizes the southwestern deserts, the Interior West—sudden downpours of rain, surprising flash floods, hidden trickles of water in mountain canyons, explosions of quail from thickets of mesquite. Spadefoot toads emerge from underground retreats within an hour of the first heavy summer rains; they call and mate in the short-lived pools. Pronghorn, usually found on grassland and sagebrush in more humid environments, roam the arid landscapes of extreme southwestern Arizona. Jackrabbits, or black-tailed hares, may be the most commonly seen mammal in the drier parts of the Interior West, but their appearance always comes as a surprise to the auto traveler: They appear suddenly from the cover of desert shrubs, bound beside the speeding car, and abruptly bolt back into the brush. Especially unexpected is the occasional jaguar, largest cat of the Americas, inhabitant of tropical forests, which wanders northward from Mexico into the mountains and deserts of Arizona, one as recently as 1987. May nature remain so wild and unexpected!

to live, noting particular strengths in the arts and recreation.

But hidden within this high total ranking are hints that all is not well in this "spiny and superheated" paradise. The "good life" quite beyond economic well-being seems to be threatened by the flood of newcomers who are attracted to Tucson for its amenities. While we were in town, a letter to the editor appeared in the *Arizona Daily Star* from late author Edward Abbey (1982)—resident of Tucson—who suggested that "excessive growth is an unhealthy, pathological, and finally, a cancerous condition [that will make] Tucson a foul mess like Phoenix." Sonnichsen (1982) was more gentle but may agree with Abbey's nostalgic regret: "The 1920's, from some points of view, were the best years Tucson ever had—perhaps the best she would ever have. . . . The town was big enough to be called a city, but not too big to keep its community spirit. It was prosperous enough, but not too prosperous. Its rich people were not too rich; its poor people were not hopelessly poor. It was growing and developing, but not too fast." Lawrence Clark Powell (1976) expressed the same sentiment but emphasized more explicitly the loss of the Garden to Turnerian growth: "More people mean more problems. From rancheria to pueblo, frontier outpost, village, and town and still not a real city, Tucson aspires to a million inhabitants by the turn of the century. Thus it seems fated to become another metropolis, choked by traffic and smothered by dusty fumes, a city such as those, east and west, from which people fled in search of a quieter, cleaner place to live. They came to Tucson as an oasis and sanctuary. Although it is still a fair and healthful place to live and work and play, uncontrolled growth will transform it. Will this be soon?" Indeed, the low qualities of housing and education, and a high incidence of crime, so often associated with a burgeoning population, were reasons cited as pulling Tucson down in the overall ratings of the *Places Rated Almanac.*

Our impressions of Tucson were mixed. Like many tourists and new residents, we were attracted by the richness of setting and comfort of climate that bring others to the city and its environs. Like Abbey, Sonnichsen, and Powell, however, we sensed a tragic finale to Frederick Jackson Turner's play. Once departed from the rambling villas of wealthy Tucson and the better-than-average housing of mid-American Tucson, we were especially struck by the poverty in other parts of town. Modest housing that could not keep body and soul together during a northern winter characterized the neighborhoods of Tucson along u.s. 89 south of the downtown. We certainly had seen more modest, more run-down dwellings in both cit-

URBAN GROWTH. Growth of major cities in the Interior West has transformed them from "livable" settlements to crowded metropolises. Whether Albuquerque or Denver, Salt Lake City or Phoenix, Santa Fe or Tucson, such transformations suggest the problem of maintaining a Garden in a settlement that continues on the pathway of Turnerian Growth. (Cartoon copyright © 1983, John Trever, *Albuquerque Journal*)

"SO .... HARRY — AS LONG AS WE'VE GOT SOME TIME HERE, TELL US MORE ABOUT THIS BIG AWARD FOR LIVEABILITY THE CITY WON...."

ies and rural settings in other parts of the country, but somehow the little houses with boarded windows, debris-strewn yards, and attic-nesting pigeons surprised us. Perhaps our reaction reflected the failure of reality to conform to the image of paradise, of the Big Rock Candy Mountain, that seems to be so much a part of the image of Arizona.

Cutting through the new housing in affluent north Tucson, U.S. 89 swings north up the Cañada del Oro—the Canyon of Gold—and around the western end of the Santa Catalina Mountains. Seeing a last flurry of condominium construction, it heads out across a surface of pediment and alluvial fill, an "empty" arid landscape. This is not the rock and sand south of Tucson, nor the spectacular desert of dense saguaro stands commemorated in Saguaro National Monument, but a surprisingly lush vegetation of cholla and prickly pear, mesquite and creosote bush. The landscape is broad and mostly level, with mountains off in the distance. Except for the brief agricultural fields near Florence, where the highway crosses the Gila River, U.S. 89 passes through mostly undeveloped ranching land until it reaches Apache Junction, on the outskirts of Phoenix, about one hundred miles north of Tucson. The interstate freeway, farming settlements, and expanses of cotton and alfalfa remain far to the west, beside the Santa Cruz River.

Along this stretch of highway, about fifty miles north of Tucson, a large parking area signals a memorial to movie-cowboy Tom Mix. Six or seven picnic tables beneath wooden sun shelters with palm fronds for roofs—all spray-painted green (including the dried palm fronds above and the trash barrels below), suggesting the importance of this cool, rich color in such a hot, arid environment—sit beside the asphalt pavement. The focal point of the little wayside is a flat-topped, rock and concrete pyramid, capped with gold paint and supporting an outline of a saddled but riderless horse. As cactus wrens chortle in the background, visitors may read the inscription on the plaque imbedded on one side of the pyramid:

JANUARY 6, 1880—OCTOBER 12, 1940
In Memory of Tom Mix
whose spirit left his body on this spot
and whose characterization and portrayals
in life served to better fix memories of
the old west in the minds of living man.

Nowhere at the wayside does the traveler learn the circumstances of the death commemorated here: Tom Mix

6. Monument to Tom Mix, between
Oracle Junction and Florence, Arizona.

died at this spot when his green, custom Cord roadster ran off the road and overturned; he was perhaps driving too fast and apparently could not successfully maneuver onto a detour set up by a road crew.

The legend of Tom Mix attests to the desire of Americans to idealize the cowboy of the Frontier and the mythical life that he led and leads. The "real" Tom Mix was born into a Pennsylvania lumbering family, dropped out of school after the fourth grade, never saw combat action in the U.S. Army but was "officially listed as a deserter in 1902," joined the Miller Brothers 101 Ranch Wild West Show, and went on to star in nearly two hundred western films. He enjoyed women, and they him. He spent his fortunes with reckless abandon. Yet, he had traits that are usually considered admirable: A recent biographer, Paul Mix (1972), suggests that "Tom's lectures on law and order, motherhood, and the American Flag were sincere on his part. . . . He sincerely believed that youngsters should be Straight Shooters in life and strive to do their best in all of their undertakings."

The same biographer almost apologizes for turning up stories about Tom Mix and his life that run counter to the legend of the Texas-born, range-raised army hero who became a cowboy star: "Many people . . . may be somewhat disillusioned by this new picture of Tom." Should the "truth" prevail, the myth be exposed? Failure to understand the world "objectively" may create problems, even crises, but mythical images, whether or not "true," may also help people to organize the world, to see meaning in existence. Maybe a critical factor in judging such myths is the degree to which they help create desirable interactions among people and between people and the land. It is true that some are critical of the movie cowboy image as fostering a domineering and aggressive macho-man with contemporary expressions in Rambo foreign policy (Kittredge 1987). Yet, others see the cinema western more positively, as a celebration of freedom and as crucial a factor in our image to the world as was the Statue of Liberty in the nineteenth century and Niagara Falls in the eighteenth. In a review of Russell Martin's book, *Cowboy: The Enduring Myth of the Wild West*, Stan Steiner (1984) suggests that the cowboy image helps to maintain a positive attitude toward a wild and unbounded western landscape: "By themselves the man and his myth do not overwhelm the mind and the senses; it is the land they represent . . . the incredible beauty and vastness of the land, the endless horizons and spaceship skies. . . . The cowboy has come to symbolize this America." If the mythical cowboy such as Tom Mix is fostering appreciation for the "beauty and vastness" of wild America, which is not unlikely, the myth is earning its worth.

Thirty miles to the north, beyond Florence, the Gila River, and the Central Arizona Project canal, the highway landscape suggests another image of the West, one not related to its "incredible beauty" but one certainly associated with its "vastness." The military services of the federal government administer large acreages of western landscape, and the Florence Military Reservation is but a small representative of that domain. The negative image that such land use engenders within the American mind about the arid West is unfortunate. Military reservations may serve a conservation function by precluding more intensive land uses—for example, the open spaces on both ends of the Golden Gate Bridge on San Francisco Bay, now much valued and protected wild landscape, are today free of houses and commercial structures because the areas had once been Army land. Moreover, such land uses generate more than a little historic interest, as witnessed by the preservation of a Titan 2 missile base near Tucson as part of the Pima Air Museum. Still, in balance, the use of so much desert for exploding bombs only contributes to the already too common negative image of arid landscape as "worthless wasteland."

Phoenix to Kanab

After swinging northwest beneath the western wall of the Superstition Mountains, the highway turns due west at Apache Junction and enters the outskirts of greater Phoenix, the largest city not only in Arizona but also anywhere along U.S. 89. The urban area also marks the end of the long, gradual descent from Nogales; after rising and falling almost imperceptibly between Tucson and Apache Junction, U.S. 89 reaches its lowest elevation in downtown Phoenix at about 1000 feet above sea level. The broad, flat plain on which sprawl the city and its satellite settlements—Mesa, Tempe, Scottsdale, Glendale—is the hottest and driest place anywhere along the route. The locals call it, with good reason, "The Valley of the Sun."

The popular name of this expansive lowland was not the only thing that made us think of its Desert character. Cacti were featured as foundation plantings in landscape nurseries. Palm trees towered above the low buildings. Canals flowed beside and beneath the broad streets. But perhaps more impressive was the absence of features prominent in a more humid environment: rows of large shade trees, expanses of lush lawns, weeds on road shoulders, water in the city's river. Yet, in comparison to the bare gravel soils and scattered low, sparsely foliated shrubs in Papago Park, the surrounding city of Phoenix seemed a prosperous contradiction to the Desert, even an emphatic denial of aridity.

The city is named after the mythical bird, the phoenix, which is destroyed by fire every five hundred years and yet rises again from its own ashes. Early agriculturalist Darrel Duppa observed the prehistoric and abandoned canals built and used by the Hohokam people to move water from the Salt River into their agricultural fields in the first century A.D.; praising the agricultural potential of the area, he suggested that "a city will rise Phoenix-like, new and more beautiful from these ashes of the past." The euphoria of the vision may reflect, as some have reported, Duppa's being blind drunk when he named Phoenix.

But indeed, a city has "risen." Unlike Tucson, which has a long and colorful history of Indian and Hispanic influences, Phoenix's past is just the opposite—the American Guide Series book on Arizona observes that "the present city . . . has developed within the span of one human life," and it has "prided itself as being a 'purely American town'" (Writers' Program 1940). Hay was first harvested in the area in 1864, and by 1868 entrepreneurs like Duppa had cleared out the silt and sand that clogged the old Indian canals and were irrigating crop land; a small settlement based on irrigated agriculture soon followed. Cities adjacent to Phoenix, notably Mesa and Glendale, started as Mormon settlements and were also agriculturally based. The subsequent population growth, first associated with agriculture and later with mines, military, and manufacturing, was remarkable. From 300 people in 1870 and 3000 in 1890, Phoenix averaged about 6 percent growth per year over the next century; in the 1950s much of this expansion was accomplished by annexation of already populated areas, but over its brief history, Phoenix has grown mostly by in-migration. Today, it encompasses a population of nearly 900,000 within its city limits and a total of almost two million in its urban area. Whether seen from a distance on South Mountain or up close along U.S. 89, greater Phoenix is impressive for its immense spread of low buildings, its shopping centers, its regular grid pattern of streets.

7. Tempe Canal and city limit of Mesa, in greater Phoenix urban area.

As was true for Tucson, growth in metropolitan Phoenix has fed, and continues to feed, at least in part, on the images of the Garden and the Playground. In the *Phoenix Sun* for New Year's Day, 1984, a story reported the great success of the Fiesta Bowl parade (a celebration held in Tempe) because it "plugged nationwide" the glories of the state. One of the hosts for the televised parade was quoted as a particularly effective Arizona booster: "Happy New Year from sun-drenched Phoenix, a vacation paradise year around with more five star resorts than any other state. More golf courses, more tennis, more things to see and do. Plus more swimming pools in one place. Certainly more popular than snowshoes are back East this time of year. And it's this warm-weather resort living that is attracting more people to Arizona each year" (LaJeunesse 1984).

One Boston visitor would apparently disagree with such a paradisiacal vision of Phoenix: "To an Easterner, Phoenix does not appear to be a city at all. It's mostly empty space divided up by traffic jams . . . . three or four rock buttes and six or eight tall hotels and office buildings.

8. Old and new in downtown Phoenix, Arizona, on Monroe Street between 3rd and 4th avenues. The church is on the site of the "first Catholic Church to serve the Phoenix area," dedicated in 1881. The contemporary high-rise of glass is the Valley Center.

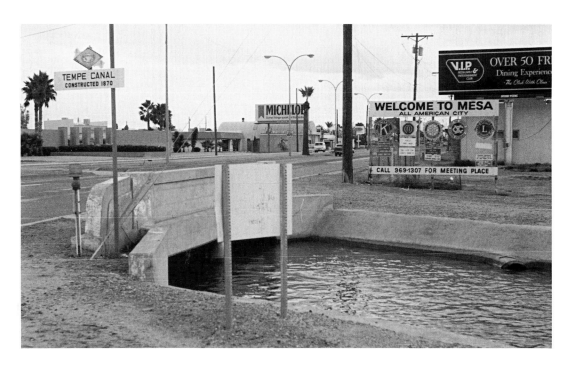

Everything else is a kind of mangy groundcover of bunga-
lows, shopping strips, automobiles, and scrub cactus . . . .
Robert Frost said that writing free verse is like playing tennis without a net. Phoenix is like that—a city without constraints, and therefore, without form" (Campbell 1983).

We, too, observed the traffic move heavily and fast
through this human-made paradise, the smog hanging
heavy in the dry desert air. Moreover, we had experienced
a particularly poignant instance of disillusionment. We
had often admired the orange trees, laden with colorful
fruit, which occasionally lined U.S. 89—they seemed a
symbol of the bounty of the Valley of the Sun—and we
wondered why such a harvest was not reaped. Indeed, it
would be almost as difficult to quench one's thirst from
this fruit as from the fantastical "lemonade springs" on
the Big Rock Candy Mountain. The trees, we learned, are
of an ornamental variety, and the fruit is inedible.

To what extent is the Garden image of Phoenix an illusion? The urban concentration has been made possible
only by the availability of water. Unlike Tucson, which
depends entirely upon groundwater, Phoenix has a surface
water supply. The Salt River, which drains much of the
mountainous land east and north of town, provided water
for both the Hohokam and early Anglo farmers. The latter
tapped the river informally with low diversion dams and
simple canals leading away from the stream. By the turn
of the century, the demands placed upon the unregulated
river became apparent: In 1891, warm rains and melting
snow caused the Salt River to wash out some of the irrigation facilities and to flood much of the southern part of
Phoenix. At the end of that same decade, from 1897 to
1899, too little rainfall brought farmers into armed conflict as they quarreled over the meager water supply. The
federal Reclamation Act, approved by Congress in 1902,
provided the means of resolving the problem of an unpredictable water resource. The water users in the greater
Phoenix area banded together as the Salt River Valley
Water Users' Association, used their lands as security, and
received federal loans for water projects on the Salt River.
The Roosevelt Dam, started in 1905 and completed in
1912, was the key element in the development, although
other dams followed. Serious pumping of ground water
started after World War II, and it now accounts for about
one-third of the water used in the Salt River Project area.
The Desert of the Valley of the Sun was thus transformed
into a Garden, a Middle Landscape, and some of it subse-

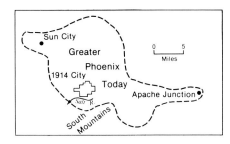

PHOENIX. In 1914, the city of Phoenix
lay in a small area immediately north
of South Mountain and the Salt River.
Today, the old city is the downtown
for a suburban and commercial region
more than fifty miles long.

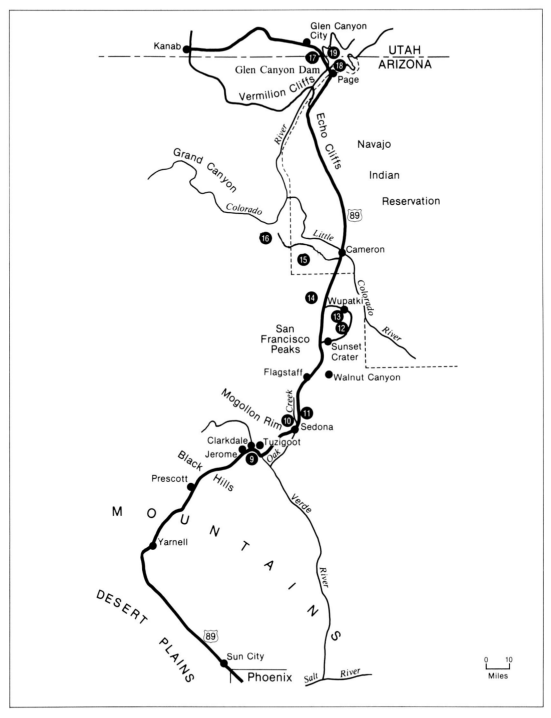

PHOENIX TO KANAB

quently moved along the Turnerian pathway to the modern city.

Does this perspective include a completion of Turner's directional vision of progress, a climax of stagnation or disaster? Some suggest that excessive water use, use exceeding supply, will cause the downfall of Phoenix and much of central Arizona. Two recent efforts have been designed to counter that downfall. The Central Arizona Project, intended to move water from the Colorado River at Lake Havasu, addresses the issue by attempting to increase supplies of water; a typical American, perhaps human, response to shortages is to increase supply rather than to learn to live with less. Approved by Congress in 1968, the CAP is a multibillion dollar project that is now delivering water to Phoenix and Tucson. The 1980 Groundwater Management Act takes a different tack; it is designed to make possible state constraints on groundwater use. The law provides for state actions, including mandatory conservation measures and purchase of agricultural land, to achieve zero overdraft levels by the year 2025 in the regions that have experienced serious groundwater depletion. The increased supplies from the Colorado River will reduce groundwater overdrafts by only half, and thus urban water uses will require conservation practices and irrigated agriculture will likely be reduced. The last point is probably the key: Ironically, for those admirers of the Garden, the transformation of irrigated agricultural fields into city streets and row houses may make possible a persistence of human society in the Valley of the Sun because such land uses require less water.

Yet, the image of the Big Rock Candy Mountain still beckons. Certainly the palatial homes that flank Camelback Mountain are no illusion. Such a show of opulence continues to generate envy, perhaps angry envy, among the unemployed, the homeless, the wanderers. Such transients, carrying their belongings in backpacks or in commandeered shopping carts, commonly trudge along the Phoenix streets of U.S. 89. Economic prosperity does not appear within their grasp, and the newspapers carry their stories. The city did not know what to do with the unusually large numbers of transients. Private aid centers cannot help everyone, and the public facilities are limited. Thus, in the mid–1980s, when the United States generally was enjoying economic prosperity, people were forced to live in "shacks of scrap wood and palm fronds at Tent City, two lots at Ninth Avenue and Jefferson, huddling around fires and bitterly denouncing the city's lack of preparedness" (Hall 1983). Others were staying in Liberty Park in downtown Phoenix. Still others found shelter beneath the 7th Avenue Bridge. In 1983, mayor-elect Terry Goddard was promising new city shelters; meanwhile, Tucson mayor Lewis Murphy thought that the program would only encourage down-and-outers to flock to Phoenix, and he did not envision such aid at Tucson: "[The transients] murder each other. They rape our citizens. They intimidate and coerce our shopowners, including extortion. That type of anti-social lawbreaking activity is just not going to be tolerated in Tucson, Arizona" (Hall 1983).

Most of these transients are locals, but the jobless continue to be drawn into Phoenix because of its image as a place of economic opportunity: "Three weeks ago, 60-year-old Wilbur Denton and his wife, Jacqueline, arrived in Phoenix in their bashed-in 1971 Pontiac. . . . They came from Omaha, Nebraska, looking for work, having heard the economy is booming in Phoenix and work is plentiful. . . . 'It was so easy to find a job here 10 years ago that we thought we would have no problems. How wrong we were. Finding a cheap place to live here now is something else.'" A worker at the St. Vincent de Paul Transient Aid Center encapsulated the motivation of such people: "[The] Dentons' story is common. Many families come to Phoenix with the hopes of finding employment, only to be disappointed. People think this is El Dorado" (Ariav 1984). How reminiscent of the Spanish explorers centuries ago!

Anyone who spends many hours driving and walking the streets of greater Phoenix will realize that El Dorado exists for only the elite of Camelback Mountain and Scottsdale. We were impressed with the contrast between rich and poor that was greater here than in Tucson. As we left the city, the memories of plywood lean-tos among cacti lingered longer than those of swimming pools near the golf courses. If the water supply will not stop the growth of Phoenix, perhaps the economic system will do so. Will the legend of the phoenix prove as foreboding for the next century of Phoenix as it was promising for the past century?

From the north edge of Phoenix, u.s. 89 heads northwest. It passes by the retirement community of Sun City, and, paralleling the Santa Fe Railroad tracks, gradually rises up a long, gently sloping plain of cotton fields. As the elevation increases, the desert vegetation becomes richer in cacti and mesquite, and generally appears more luxuriant. About sixty miles beyond Phoenix, the high-way turns sharply northeast and climbs up a spectacular grade to the 5000-foot elevation of Yarnell. From the top of the grade, we stopped to look back over the desert sweeping away to the south. The winds carried to us faintly the songs of cactus wrens from below.

For now, the desert is left behind and the road crosses an upland landscape that is different from areas farther south in both natural and cultural features. This mountainous area belongs to the basin and range region, but its mountain ridges are compacted together into a "jumbled aggregate having little . . . symmetry" (Comeaux 1981). Thick stands of brush cover the steep slopes of the sometimes rugged terrain, and grass appears in the broad valleys; as the highway climbs into still higher elevations, ponderosa pine gives the land a Western mountain appearance.

The landscape is one of ranches and cattle, although its historical roots are in mining. The major settlement of this part of Arizona, the "mile-high-city" of Prescott, orig-inated as a mining community in the 1860s. The town flourished and for a time even served as the state capital. But isolated from major transportation corridors and walled in by broken terrain, Prescott never developed as did Phoenix. Nonetheless, its diversified economic base of ranching, mining, logging, and government services has kept Prescott a busy, medium-sized town. In fact, it ap-peals so much to the residents of the urban centers to the south that it now serves as a vacation and retirement com-munity for those wishing to escape the crowds and heat. Homesites and tourist businesses are conspicuous not only in town but also in the surrounding valleys crossed by the highway. Is Turnerian development transforming Prescott into a sprawling, congested city, not of "the man-ufacturing organization . . . [or the] factory system," but of the Playground?

The potential is present for another small town to lose what many would consider its quiet amenity. In Decem-ber of 1983, a proposed hotel and convention development on the Yavapai-Prescott Indian Reservation adjacent to the town and in the nearby community of Granite Dells con-cerned city business leaders because they feared loss of economic activity in the downtown—such developments on the periphery of Phoenix have turned its downtown into what has been called a "deserted wasteland." In ad-dition, environmental effects of a growing, sprawling city worry environmentalists who point out that even in Pres-

DESERT. The desert of the extreme southwestern United States is usually subdivided into a slightly higher elevation Mojave Desert, where cool winter temperatures and snowfall are not uncommon, and a lower and warmer Sonoran Desert. Bailey (1978) merges the two into the American Desert and perhaps with reason: The entire region is dominated by the ubiquitous creosote bush, often in large expanses of nearly pure stands but also with other low shrubs and the more upright mesquite or saguaro or Joshua Tree. Black-throated sparrows and Le Conte's thrashers sing from perches on the woody plants. Nocturnal, burrowing rodents are the most common mammals, preyed upon by kit foxes, coyotes, and birds of prey. Species of lizards and snakes are unusually numerous. By whatever name, this desert region is rich with life.

cott groundwater overdrafts are lowering the water table.

Still, as of yet, Prescott projects the image of the early stages of Turner's views on development. Prescott plays on its cowboy, Western ranch image, boasting of its rodeo, the first public rodeo in the United States. The courthouse square is bordered by stores that offer "western ware." On the square itself, sits an impressive statue of "Buckey" O'Neill, a local who died in the Spanish-American War and who takes on heroic characteristics as "a 'first-rate fighting man,' happiest in the pursuit of outlaws, and always ready to risk a chance with either bullets or cards." An adjacent business street identifies itself as the remnants of "Whisky Row," a line of old "saloons" that were, except for two, destroyed by fire in 1900, allegedly started by a drunken miner who tipped over a kerosene lamp. A new shopping center in Chino Valley, north of the downtown, attempts to capture the Frontier image with its low, wooden buildings fronted by wooden overhangs above the sidewalks, but it mixes the images of Hispanic tradition, the Deep South, and the Cowboy West with its admonition to return: "Adios, podner! Y'all come back soon! Ya hear!" This small town's Frontier feeling seemed to appeal not only to us and to the Arizonan from Phoenix or Mesa, but also to the out-of-stater: In a 1984, informal rating of the "most desirable medium-sized towns of America," Prescott came in number one.

Across Chino Valley, a wide grassland dotted with scattered wooden frame houses and occasional small herds of pronghorn antelope, u.s. 89 again plunges into mountains. Winding up a forested canyon of the Black Hills, it reaches a 7000-foot summit before descending sharply on the east side. The road pokes its way through a narrow notch between high rock cliffs and enters a distinctive mining settlement, formerly proclaimed in grammatical exuberance, "The Most Unique City in America."

Jerome clings to the steep slopes of the Black Hills as they rise precipitously from the Verde River Valley. The description from the American Guide Series book on Arizona seems apt: "[Its] frame houses [are] a jumble on stilts. With a fifteen-hundred-foot difference in elevation between the highest and lowest perches, the town has some houses with basements reached by a climb up three flights of steps, others with roofs below the level of the streets on which they face, and yet others with garages on their roofs. Many householders can lean out of their kitchen windows and scratch matches on their neighbors' chimneys."

The town was built in response to the mineral wealth of the adjacent slopes. The "big rock" in this mountain was copper, which was mined from underground shafts and open pits almost continuously from 1882 to 1953. The ore was so concentrated and so abundant that it supported the richest individually owned copper mine in the world. By 1900, Jerome was one of the largest settlements in Arizona, and in 1929 it had a population of fifteen thousand. After the Second World War, production declined and then ceased; the town was largely abandoned.

Today, Jerome has enjoyed a rebirth; some might say it is being unfortunately gentrified. Restaurants, antique shops, trinket outlets, and artists occupy some of the old buildings. Like Prescott, Jerome benefits from tourist interest in the Frontier West. The population has even grown to about four hundred, maybe twice the number who lived there in 1960. Yet, this is no Virginia City, no Telluride; Jerome's unpainted and unkempt look, its washed-out roads and overgrown lots, its quiet and loneliness, poignantly maintain the aura of an abandoned mining town.

The typical American affection for ghost towns is curious. A sense of heroic human endeavor permeates that reaction: "The history of Jerome is a story of tough men against a rough mountain. It's a hard story of hard rock, hard work, hard liquor, and hard play. . . . Jerome [is taking] its rightful place among the picturesque old towns of the once roaring West—a great out-door museum dedicated to its own marvelous story of mines, men, and money. [The] element that really sets Jerome apart is the colorful and exciting saga of the men who burrowed deep in the mountains. . . . They came from the town's beginning until its decline, men and women of many countries and classes, and they boosted, boomed, and built the first lonely camp into a town and the town into a clamoring little city" (Brewer 1983).

Jerome is not unique in generating this sort of admiration. Throughout the American West, towns that have failed when the mines have failed generate devoted followings—Bodie and Belmont, Elkhorn and Florence, Virginia City, Georgetown, and Cripple Creek; the list could go on and on. Books are devoted to them; post cards feature them; maps locate them; state parks protect them; tourists flock to them; amusement parks create them. Americans have made their past, especially their Western past, heroic, and thus the towns of that past have become a celebrated part of it.

9. Jerome, hanging on the mountain slope above the Verde Valley. The cliff in the distance is the Mogollon Rim, southern edge of the Colorado Plateau physiographic region.

Yet, while they prospered, the towns often were a concentration of vile activities that few today would tolerate, much less admire, in their own hometowns. The fumes from the copper smelters at Jerome, for example, killed the forest that once covered the slopes above the town. The water draining the tailings must have produced the worst of pollutions in the valley below. Blasting in the mines contributed to the instability of the slopes and thus encouraged the sliding of the town's buildings into ruin. Lax attitudes toward public safety allowed the town to burn repeatedly during the 1890s. Tolerance for various vices allowed Jerome to develop a reputation typical for such a settlement: "[Lights] blazed all night in Jerome's never closing taverns and restaurants and houses of pleasure. . . . Miners and smeltermen poured down the hill at intervals night and day, to join in activities which made an observer wonder if there might not be truth in the widely circulated story that Jerome was the wickedest city in America" (Young 1972).

Americans seem to like that image of towns of the past, but express regret, or outrage, at such activities in settlements of today. The coal mines of Appalachia are scorned as polluters and despoilers, and the boom towns of Wyoming, like Rock Springs and Gillette, are portrayed as hellholes of crime and prostitution and uncontrolled growth. Mining towns seem to be unusual, perhaps unique, among American settlements in being problems when they are booming but desirable when they have failed. Just as Americans have created romantic heroes out of their movie cowboys like Tom Mix, so too have they remade into romantic sagas the histories of their early mining towns.

After switchbacking through lower Jerome, U.S. 89 heads across the broad Verde Valley, still within the mountains and still at a fairly high elevation of more than three thousand feet. Rich in water, this lowland—the largest northern watershed of the Salt River—supports ranches and clusters of settlements that originated when copper smelting was the dominant activity in the valley's major town of Clarkdale. Along the river, Tuzigoot National Monument commemorates a still older settlement, a twelfth-century, twenty-room, hilltop dwelling of the Hohokam/Sinagua people. As we approached Tuzigoot, driving between colorful old tailing spoils of the copper days, we assumed that the low walls were indeed a ruin of the original building; even the Park Service leaflet describes the monument as saving "a remnant of a prehistoric town." Yet, nothing of the former structure survived into the modern day, and the low walls that visitors see were reconstructed in the 1930s after archaeological investigations were completed. The "ruin" was built not only to give visitors something definite to view but also to give them the illusion of seeing something ancient. How many tourists at Tuzigoot think that those walls are as original as the wooden walls of Jerome?

After crossing the Verde River, U.S. 89 angles north and east and heads toward the high sandstone cliffs of the Mogollon Rim, the southern edge of the Colorado Plateau. For five hundred miles, U.S. 89 cuts northward across this physiographic region. At first amid forests of ponderosa pine, then atop vast arid plains with distant towering cliffs, and finally through high mountain valleys, the highway rarely loses sight of colorful rocks—tan and yellow and pink and white and, especially, red. The Colorado Plateau is anything but bland.

At the base of the Mogollon Rim sits the town of Sedona. Founded by colonizing Mormons as an agricultural town, Sedona today serves as an arts and crafts center, a

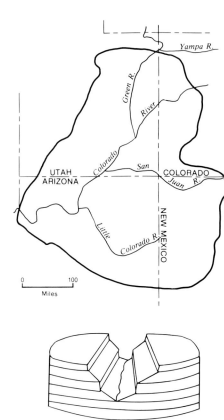

COLORADO PLATEAU. The Colorado Plateau region has been likened to a great stack of flat plates, each of which is a bed of limestone, or sandstone, or siltstone, all uplifted as a group without greatly violating their horizontal inclination. Throughout the region, streams have downcut through the stack and exposed in cross section the individual rock layers, thereby producing the rugged and colorful canyons for which the Colorado Plateau is famous. In some places the rock layers are locally broken by faults or twisted by folds, which add to the great relief produced by stream incision. For many, the Colorado Plateau represents the ideal blending of the arid and mountainous West. (Map adapted from Hunt 1974)

retirement and vacation home center, a tourist town. It, as much as any town along the route so far, promotes its Garden image as a Playground. Its spectacular topographic setting combined with Oak Creek rushing along a rocky channel and a mild but four-season climate makes Sedona seem like still another Arizona Eden. It has sometimes been described as "the most beautiful town in America"; a local writer describes it as a "modern-day Shangri-La."

As tourists, we wandered in "uptown Sedona," the small cluster of motels, shops, taverns, and restaurants directly beneath the red rock cliffs in what seemed to be the oldest part of the settlement. The relatively new "arts and crafts village" of Tlaquepaque presented an intricate adobe-like building of walkways, staircases, porches, and courtyards, decorated by stone driveways, arched doorways, wrought-iron railings, water fountains, and red-tile roofs. But the newer subdivisions seemed carelessly sprawled out over the wooded plain to the south, and the commercial strip of "west Sedona" seemed anything but special.

Modern Sedona definitely did not seem like Shangri-La to author Page Stegner (1981). He was a schoolboy resident in Sedona in the early 1950s when he fondly considered the town to be a "gas and cigs quick stop." In 1981 he did not recognize the place: "Where am I? I creep along for about a mile, past a continuous strip of gift shops, real estate offices, motels, restaurants, cocktail lounges, craft centers, art galleries, boutiques, Indian pottery, baskets, jewelry, kachinas, sand paintings, pawn, hand-crafted this, authentic that, unusual, exclusive, unique. It suddenly occurs to me that I am here. Sedona. My town trip. . . . What chance does (did) a little town with a population of six thousand (fifty-five hundred more than when I first saw it) stand against a tourist influx of over two million people a year? When one out of every twenty residents is a real estate agent, what else is going to proliferate except real estate development?"

As with the other nirvanas through which U.S. 89 has already passed, this one called Sedona is threatened by growth, according to Stegner. But did the residents of Sedona in 1950 resent the coming of Page Stegner as much as he resents the coming of those since? Are there no absolutes in the regret with which Americans view landscape change and the nostalgia with which they view the past? Still, this observation does not make unimportant reactions such as that of Stegner: The idealization of the past may be a positive force, rather than a fatalistically

10. Construction of new retail stores on "the strip" of south Sedona. In spite of the regionally appropriate, southwestern-style adobe appearance of these buildings, such growth threatens the Garden image of Sedona.

negative and simply sentimental one, if it helps a society to define what sorts of landscapes it chooses to value, to preserve, and to develop.

The nostalgic regret which Page Stegner expresses is not an isolated reaction of a one-time, long-ago resident who has returned to a place he once knew. Others in Sedona have seen the change generated by growth as a threat, and yet seem unable to embrace a no-growth world. According to the local newspaper, the Yavapai County planning agency and the county board of supervisors denied a plan for an enlarged market, pending completion of a report on commercial development in the west side of Sedona, although that same county board had approved a large commercial and residential complex in the same area. A companion, front-page story reported the denial by the Coconino County planning agency (Sedona sits astride a county line) to allow the enlargement of an existing motel near the mouth of Oak Creek Canyon on the other side of town, even though the bigger motel would be remodeled with an "architectural style . . . more . . . 'southwestern.'" In contrast, that same board approved the rezoning of sixty-four acres to allow the construction of over one hundred new single-family homes. The ambivalence obviously felt by the local governmental bodies was reflected in comments on the editorial page. A letter to the editor talked of the need to preserve "the area's attributes" but still spoke of "the inevitable growth" of the community. Moreover, the main editorial column hinted that it was "time for change" in the ways in which the open lands around Sedona are used because so many towns-people are more accustomed to a "suburban type of living" than to an "open range" lifestyle; the two incidents which prompted this questioning involved "a trapper whose traps near town [had] caught a pet or two, and a cattleman whose stock [grazed] their way into town" (*Red Rock News* 1983). Does Sedona's 1987–1988 incorporation as a city, reportedly prompted as a measure necessary to institute growth controls, portend genuine "progress against growth," to use Daniel Luten's apt phrase (in Vale 1986), or will the prideful chests of the new city leaders swell at the thought of just one more subdivision, just one more "southwestern" style motel?

The highway leaves Sedona by following Oak Creek, the stream that the town straddles, into the massive sandstone that provides the backdrop for jewelry stores and art galleries, the fast-food restaurants and motels. For a dozen miles, the road gently winds beneath the high, reddish and whitish, near-vertical walls, sometimes forested and sometimes bare, of Oak Creek Canyon. We passed by small Forest Service campgrounds barricaded for the winter, a lodge or two, mostly empty, a few stores and restaurants, either closed or little used, and a scattering of small, old private vacation homes, all quiet. The leafless sycamores and dark green conifers seemed appropriate for the restful scene, as did the low flow of the creek, softly falling over the large, rounded boulders in its bed.

But our cool-season impressions belied the crowded frenzy of Oak Creek Canyon in summer. People jam themselves into this narrow cleft during the warm months, when the inviting waters of the stream and the cool shade of the trees beckon residents from the hot desert cities farther south or travelers from almost anywhere. They come to Oak Creek Canyon, not to experience a landscape transformed into a Middle Landscape and not to sense a link to the Frontier past, but to use the landscape to generate thrills and excitement, to make the landscape a Playground. The most heavily used part of the canyon is a slab of inclined, slick rock over which both the stream and vacationers slide into a deep pool. They wait in long lines to experience the cooling thrill. So many come, in fact, that restrictions have been placed on their use of the streamside landscape, as the signs in the

photo indicate: "No glass containers or bottles . . . no pets
. . . no camping . . . no fires." Even more suggestive of the
crowds that use Oak Creek Canyon is the sign warning of
pollution: "Bacteria counts often exceed state standards
for safe swimming water when more than 250 swimmers
use Slide Rock." As in Phoenix, the ready availability of
water may be an illusion, and the shortness of supply here
seems to threaten the persistence of many Playground
uses of the landscape.

At the head of the canyon, the highway climbs in a series of spectacular switchbacks to the top of the plateau,
here capped with lava, and then makes a beeline through
the great forest of ponderosa pine that characterizes the
higher elevations of northern Arizona. Rising ahead are
the San Francisco Peaks, a volcanic mountain mass built
from successive eruptions that began over two million
years ago. A subsequent explosion on the mountain flank
caused the upper slopes to collapse back in on themselves,
much like that on Mount Saint Helens. Nonetheless, one
of the remaining peaks, Humphreys Peak, is the highest
point in Arizona at 12,670 feet above sea level. More than
the ranges farther south, the towering and snowy San
Francisco Peaks befit the mental image of the West's rugged terrain. They also represent the special feeling that
people everywhere have for mountains: The San Francisco
Peaks are sacred to the Hopi and Navajo, who believe that
the kachinas reside on their heights.

At the southern base of the San Francisco Peaks and
several miles north of the tip of the Mogollon Rim, u.s.
89 enters the busy streets of Flagstaff. Since a group of
scouts camped beside Antelope Spring and raised their
homemade flag on a tall pine hewn of its branches in
1876, Flagstaff has been an oasis for travelers, first on overland trails, then on the railroad, then in autos and trucks.
Its busy railroad tracks, its fringes of roadside commercial
strips, and its busy summer streets attested to the importance of transportation functions. But Flagstaff could not
be dismissed as "just" a crowded, characterless town.
Names of tourist businesses hinted of both the Frontier
West (Black Bart's RV Park and the Stockman's Club) and
the Big Rock Candy Mountain (the Turquoise Nugget
Trading Post), but neither image seemed strong. The city's
setting amid a green forest, abutting the San Francisco
Peaks, snow-streaked even in summer, suggested a blending of the natural and the cultural, a Middle Landscape.
Strengthening this image, on the northern edge of town,
well below these rising forested slopes and snow-dappled

11. Oak Creek Canyon. The sign in the
foreground warns of unsafe bacteria
levels when Oak Creek is filled with
water-seeking visitors, a reminder to
the traveler that water is meager in
the western Desert.

peaks, sat a rural housing development called Fernwood Estates. A warm wind swayed the young planted trees, and a meadowlark sang nearby. The modest ranch-style houses were scattered along curving and dead-end streets named Sunset Boulevard, Peaks Parkway, Sunflower Lane. Corrals enclosed horses in backyards; birdbaths beckoned birds in front yards. Nevertheless, the scene was hardly as idyllic as Green Valley. Here, the lawns were sparse and unkempt, and the trees few and spindly. Perhaps most symbolic were the unoccupied birdbaths on that warm day—the residents had neglected to turn on their taps and fill them. A western garden needs more human care to blossom; a western Middle Landscape needs concern and attention—and it needs water.

Northward from Fernwood Estates, the often ephemeral status of the Western Garden became more evident. In the summer of 1983, the field of the Welfare Farm operated by the Mormon Church lay plowed but unplanted. Individual residences gradually yielded to larger lots and pastures for horse riding and boarding, then to even more open range-land apparently less and less suitable for human habitation. Fences constructed of local building materials such as large logs spanning sturdy posts of rock masonry suggested an earlier frontier.

Just to the east of the San Francisco Peaks rises the desolate cinder cone of Sunset Crater. Only because of the history presented in a Flagstaff Chamber of Commerce folder would most tourists identify this as an early site of human occupancy. The pamphlet presents a scenario suggesting the dependence of human populations upon availability of water, a familiar theme along this southern stretch of U.S. 89. It describes a possible "prehistoric land rush" when fertile, moist land became available after a volcanic eruption, the same eruption that built Sunset Crater, nine hundred years ago. While the rich, porous ash trapped whatever moisture was available, the Sinagua Indians (literally, people "without water," as coined by archaeologists) were able to grow their corn in this dry environment; but when the ash blew away or excessively long droughts failed to replenish the water supply, these early inhabitants were forced to plant their gardens elsewhere until the cycle was repeated. One such relocation site was Walnut Canyon, east of Flagstaff; today, its stream is dry, having been diverted as a water source for the city. This story is reminiscent of the legend behind the name of Phoenix, and perhaps here a longer view of American Western history suggests a cyclical concept of cul-

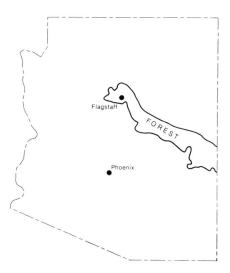

WESTERN FORESTS. The band of forest that extends east-west through the high elevations astride the Mogollon Rim is dominated by cone-bearing trees, conifers. Such trees characterize the mountain forests of the American West, presumably because their evergreen needles maximize photosynthesis during the short growing season yet protect them during the long cold winters. Pines, spruces, firs, hemlocks—they make mountain forests look Western.

12. Sunset Crater, a cone of volcanic ash. The parking lot and contact building are services provided by the National Park Service for visitors to this National Monument. The trees are mostly ponderosa pine.

tural landscape development, rather than the simple linear perspective of historian Turner. Past or present, water is a rare and precious commodity in this Desert.

Sunset Crater also suggested the Interior West as Playground. In Oak Creek Canyon, it was Slide Rock that attested to the American ingenuity in transforming almost any natural feature into a recreational instrument. Here, it was once the unlikely downslope of the cinder cone that provided the raw material for a Playground. After tediously ascending the trail to the top, some visitors delighted in racing downward, eventually eroding trenches as wide as thirty feet and as deep as ten. But in contrast to Oak Creek Canyon, where thrill-seeking amusement is promoted as an appropriate use to attract tourists, here, in a National Monument, such activity is regarded as an inappropriate use conflicting with the preservation of wild nature. The trenching scars were visible from places as distant as Flagstaff and led to the closing of the trail in 1973. The official pamphlet today is thereby able to offer reassurance to a people concerned for nature protection that here "the spatter cones and other evidences of volcanism look as if they have barely cooled."

Eighteen miles to the north is another example of the philosophical confusion over the ideal attitude toward preservation. At Wupatki National Monument, a few miles along the Park Service road, the subject for protection is a cultural one, the ruins of a large pueblo built in the 1100s at one of the prime farming sites of the "land rush" following the 1065 Sunset Crater eruption. In the 1930s, the CWA program excavated and partially restored the old ruins. Later, when Park Service policy emphasized a "purer" type of preservation, employees tore down the handwork of the CWA crews. The booklet published by the Southwestern Parks and Monuments Association explains, "We believe the ruin as it appears today leaves one with a greater feeling of admiration for the prehistoric builders than it would with any added restoration" (*Wupatki Ruins Trail* 1982). But how does this explain the meticulous restoration at Tuzigoot National Monument, less than seventy miles southward on U.S. 89? We, personally, doubt that most visitors would lose admiration for an Indian society if Tuzigoot were to be dismantled, but feel fairly certain that future archaeologists would find intriguing such paradoxical antics by the restorers/dismantlers. A few years earlier at Fort Necessity National Monument in Pennsylvania we had seen evidence that the Park Service has still not resolved its dilemma between preserving or restoring. In the 1950s, an earlier restored version of this fort of the French and Indian War was completely re-restored when new archaeological evidence indicated an original circular shape rather than the earlier supposed rectangle. Will some future Park administrators find reason to restore the "ugly" scars on Sunset Crater to lend greater appreciation for the twentieth-century recreationist—or to preserve the filled-in trenches to inspire admiration for the nature preservationists of the same period?

Pondering this weighty problem of just how and what of history to save for posterity, we strolled along the trail beside the Wupatki ruin. Indians found this area uninhabitable after 1225 until the present Navajos moved here in about 1870. Without replenishing rains and ash, the "land rush" territory became an early site for a dust bowl. Most visitors seemed more interested in catching a glimpse of

13. Main ruin at Wupatki National Monument. The circular "amphitheater" probably served ceremonial functions. The walls on the low rise immediately beyond the amphitheater are the remains of a building which housed as many as three hundred people.

the elusive small wildlife scurrying about in the hot, sunny weather than in conjuring up cloudy images of a culture long buried in the past. Perhaps the presence of frisky mammals such as desert cottontails and sprightly birds such as black-throated sparrows and rock wrens dispelled the image of an arid environment inhospitable to humans except under special conditions of irrigation or ash falls.

Before leaving, we were drawn to eavesdrop on a lighthearted conversation between two tourists. They joked about the ruins actually being a fake, hypothesizing that they were brainstormed by some entrepreneur who viewed the scene and said to himself, "Now what we actually need here is a tourist attraction. We can say that these were living quarters, that a ball court." Certainly, this could reflect the skepticism of an easterner, unfamiliar with such a dry climate, upon being told that many of the log beams and much of the native sandstone masonry had persisted relatively intact for centuries. But perhaps it also showed a distrust of appearances that might be engendered by a trip to Tuzigoot—are the ruins remnants, reconstructions, or false fabrications?

From the open forest of ponderosa pine at Sunset Crater and the rocky swale at Wupatki, the highway heads north

toward the Colorado River. The San Francisco Peaks remain visible to the south, gradually dropping below the
horizon. The great high-voltage power lines from power
plants along the river march beside the road. The shrubs
and grass sparsely cover the bare sandy soil.

Most of this land is within the Navajo Indian Reservation, and thus would seem to belong to the Frontier West.
The opportunities to buy Indian crafts—turquoise jewelry,
clay pots, woolen blankets—abounded, although the Gem
City Indian Store was closed. Particularly numerous were
the informal family outlets: roadside stands, crudely constructed of old wooden boards and corrugated metal, or
simple, rough tables set up beside parked pickup trucks
and beneath blankets propped up for shade in the one-
hundred-degree heat. The settlement of Cameron beside
the highway crossing of the Colorado River offered a motel and "trading post," but otherwise signs of human hab-
itations were restricted to scattered Navajo homes—a few
ranch-style houses and many tarpaper shacks, old hogans,
and new mobile homes. Fences of wire and juniper enclosed corrals for goats and sheep. Shade trees were absent, and the shrubs scattered and meager. This is not an
easy land, although the tenacity of humans here suggested
that people can survive without much water. Perhaps
modern dwellers, like the old Sinagua, have a lesson for
the contemporary water-demanding cities in the Valley of
the Sun. After all, have not many writers talked about the
harmony in which Native Americans lived, and live, with
the land?

But the surprising frequency of Navajos and Navajo
homes in this dry environment suggests a different lesson
about people and their habitat. Clyde Kluckhohn and Dorothea Leighton (1946), in their classic scholarly book on
the Navajo, state that "the total productivity of the Navajo
lands has probably been reduced by at least half since 1868
. . . . [This] land destruction seems to have been acceler-
ated by uncontrolled and abusive land use, primarily overgrazing associated with overpopulation." Popular writer
Edward Abbey (1985) more bluntly indicts population
pressures by observing that "in 1890 when the Navajos
were resettled on their present reservation, they numbered about 15,000; today the tribal population is something over 160,000 and growing fast, at a rate greater than
any other American subgroup except the Hispanics and
the Mormons. In brief, the Navajos have greatly out-
bred the carrying capacity of their range. . . ." Abbey per-
ceives the overgrazing that has resulted from the increased

14. View southward at the northern edge of the forested Flagstaff upland. The volcanic mass of the San Francisco Peaks rises in the background. The high-voltage power lines carry electricity from power plants along the Colorado River into central Arizona. The Indian curio shop suggests the proximity of the Navajo Indian Reservation.

15. Navajo craftpersons and their wares in stands beside the highway to Grand Canyon National Park. The flag is the state flag of Arizona.

Navajo population as transforming a poor, "semiarid grassland to an eroded waste of blows and nettles."

Dust bowl in the 1200s and eroded waste in the 1900s—a recurrent cycle of human use and misunderstanding of this land changed our view of the arid landscape of bare rock and sand, withered low shrubs, hot and desiccating wind: The Frontier image succumbed to the Desert. We marveled at the sandstone of the Echo Cliffs towering to the east, as our tires beat on against the rough highway pavement north of Cameron—the clay in the mudstone absorbs so much water when it rains that the weathered rock heaves upward, a behavior of certain clays in dry or seasonally dry environments. We supposed that the even-hotter landscapes of southern Arizona, near Phoenix and Tucson, would have similarly evoked the Desert image had we traveled them in mid-summer. Here, though, even in June, the all-dominant drought overpowered other images. We tried to enjoy the relative coolness of early morning by searching for roadside birds, but found only several horned larks flocking beside a livestock watering tank and a few ravens flapping overhead. A coyote darted across the road, and later a slithering snake, whose successful traverse of the gauntlet of speeding vehicles seemed unusual for his kind.

A side trip to the south rim of the Grand Canyon rewarded us with spectacular views, especially of the gorge of the Little Colorado River, although haze obscured the distant vista at the Grand Canyon itself. At noon, we temporarily turned our backs on the Desert to feast on a tuna-stuffed, mango-capped avocado, which we prepared at a picnic site. A black-throated gray warbler serenaded us from a nearby piñon pine. The heat, though, won out, and we rushed on, with sixty-mile-an-hour winds blasting through our open windows and visions of a midwestern roadside rest with cool, expansive lawns and a shady forest flickering in our imaginations. But the hills between us and such relief remained ever ahead. We thought of Edward Abbey: "In this glare of brilliant emptiness, in this arid intensity of pure heat, in the heart of a weird solitude, great silence and grand desolation, all things recede to distances out of reach, reflecting light but impossible to touch, annihilating all thought and all that men have made to a spasm of whirling dust far out on the golden desert" (Abbey 1968).

One feature of "all that men have made," however, could not be ignored by Abbey, or by us, in this Desert landscape—the ubiquitous steel towers that support the

> COYOTE. Perhaps no mammal is more characteristic of the West, and especially the arid plains and plateaus of the Interior West, than the coyote. Poisoned, trapped, and shot for its image, deserved or not, as a damaging predator of domestic animals, the coyote has more than held its own. In fact, from its original distribution in areas of open vegetation west of the Mississippi River, the coyote since European settlement has expanded eastward to the Atlantic and northwestward across Canada into Alaska. Increased food supplies may have much to do with this expansion. But regardless of its more cosmopolitan range, the coyote remains a vivid symbol of the West. Whether seen on a meadow of the Yellowstone Plateau or heard on a slope of Nevada sagebrush, coyotes seem a necessary part of the American West. "May they never cease to yap on moonlight nights in the desert!" (Burt 1976).

16. Cliff and canyon at edge of Grand Canyon. A horizontal layer of hard rock defines the surface of the flat-topped mesa in the middle distance. The slopes of the mesa and the level area surrounding it support an open forest of "pygmy conifers," juniper and piñon pine.

graceful arcs of power lines as they "stride across the horizon in multicolumn grandeur, looped together by the swoop and gleam of high-voltage cables." Yet, he sees beyond such pleasant aesthetics and imagines the towers as "120-foot space monsters." Their role as symbols of the Empty Quarter seems implicit in his description of the crowded, electricity-demanding urban centers as "blazing cities feed[ing] on the defenseless interior" (Abbey 1975). The power lines along this stretch of u.s. 89 are part of the financial foundation of the Central Arizona Project, and the power that they carry comes from either the hydro facilities at Glen Canyon Dam or a coal plant at Page. They stand tall in this otherwise empty, uncluttered environment—are they emphatic exclamation marks of an impersonal industrial society defiling the wild nature of this Empty Quarter, or proud human structures offering reassurance that the Desert can be subdued, or merely graceful cultural forms that blend with the bold starkness of the natural scene in a sort of Middle Landscape?

u.s. 89 turns toward the northeast, climbs up the side of the spectacular Echo Cliffs along a series of rock blocks that have moved downward by faulting, and then races along an upland rock bench to the Colorado River, important water source for much of the American Southwest. Its liquid treasures are funneled off from its headwaters to

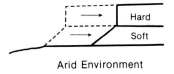

Arid Environment

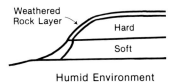

Humid Environment

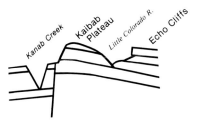

DESERT SLOPES. The high wall of the Echo Cliffs, along the base of which runs U.S. 89, is a prime example of the erosional escarpments of the Colorado Plateau. Initially created by stream incision, these regional cliff faces have eroded back through time, a backward retreat caused by the relatively rapid erosion of soft rock beneath the hard, cliff-forming rock layer. In a humid environment, a thick covering of soil and weathered rock would smooth out the angular slope form. Here, the cliff is bold and prominent, spectacular testimony to its arid setting. (Bottom figure adapted from Hunt 1974)

17. Glen Canyon Dam on the Colorado River. The primary purpose of the dam is to generate electricity, and the Central Arizona Project, to which it contributes, will replace groundwater overdrafts with Colorado River water. Yet, the image-makers want to believe that a Garden is being made out of the Desert.

the High Plains, from its lower reaches to coastal southern California, from along its entire length to innumerable fields and towns close by; most recently, its waters have been taken from the reservoir of Lake Havasu to the cotton fields and swimming pools of central Arizona. The river has been dammed repeatedly for power generation, water storage, and flood control. The traveler along u.s. 89 crosses the Colorado on a steel arch bridge, just below the most recent of these dams, Glen Canyon.

Glen Canyon Dam stands as the greatest symbol of the greatest natural resource controversy in the American West: water development. The issue had been simply whether or not the dam should be built and, once completed, whether or not the reservoir behind it should be filled. Congressional hearings over these questions packed volumes; glossy publications extolled the beauty of the natural, vertical-walled canyon, now gone from sight, and of the deep-blue lake that obliterated it; advocates of the project have defended it as a glory of modern engineering, while critics have fantasized about "just one crack." Condensed to its fundamentals, the argument over Glen Canyon and its dam was based on different images of the West. On one side were the Empty Quarter pressures from cities for electricity and the U.S. Congress for revenues, aided by Arizona farmers' visions of an irrigated Middle Landscape; on the other side were the forces urging protection for the beauty of the wild river and canyon. As we viewed the completed, functioning dam, we lamented having lost to us forever the opportunity to explore firsthand the mysteries and beauties of the famed, buried upstream canyon, but nevertheless found the monolithic mass of concrete, shimmering in sunlight and shadow, to be an impressive structure. We admired its massiveness, its clean, smooth form, and its overflow, unprecedented in volume, thundering out of pipes which tunnel water around the dam through the rock walls of the canyon.

All historical sense of the controversy over the dam vanishes as a tourist enters the portal of the neat, modern, lawn-bordered visitor center on the west side of the bridge. Instead, the exhibits portray the last twenty years as if time began when Congress authorized the project in 1956. Nothing before that year seems to matter—the empty spot became a place only when the dam project started. The paintings that adorned one corner of the museum showed the canyon after the dam and reservoir, but not before. The books for sale at the counter included only one Edward Abbey title, *Desert Solitaire*, a nonfiction work that lauds the amenities of this desert landscape. No opportunity was provided for the visitor to thumb through one of his later books, *The Monkey Wrench Gang*, a 1975 novel that begins with a fantasy about blowing up the arch bridge and even the dam. The exhibits telling the story of the dam's construction and the power plant tour offering a closer look at its operation each seem to suggest that the project had been built primarily for tourists, not for the generation of electricity. Was this facility an Eiffel Tower monument to human engineering? A Space Needle spectacle for observing distant vistas, complete with viewing platforms? An Epcot Center or Disneyland amusement center with elevator rides, walking tours, and slide shows?

Maybe our sense of the tourist function of the dam was close to the point. Perhaps the construction of the dam had as much to do with an unconscious sense of creation as with a conscious need to generate electricity. Glen Canyon Dam may reflect an emotional vision of the West and its place in American society as much as a practical concern for kilowatt hours, for, practically speaking, the dam at Glen Canyon serves only a "cash-register" function for the Central Arizona Project. By law, the electric power generated at the dam, as at other dams built by the Bureau of Reclamation, can be sold for revenues that help pay for the water delivery system which moves water into the regions around Phoenix and Tucson. If other means of financing had been arranged, the need for the dam would have evaporated as rapidly as water from the surface of the reservoir on a hot summer day. Such flexibility was employed later when a coal-fired power plant was constructed at the town of Page instead of hydroelectric dams in the Grand Canyon. But no such bureaucratic imagination was used here and the Glen Canyon Dam was built. Perhaps Congress needed, and still needs, even greater imagination, because there is nothing innate or natural about the seventy-five-year-old policy of subsidizing major water developments with sales of electric power. This policy simply reflects a vision that the arid West can be transformed into a Middle Landscape, a Garden, and subsequently can be further transformed by Turnerian progress into urban centers, and, moreover, that these transformations are desirable "reclamations" of the Desert. Other, contrary, visions recognize physical limits, such as lack of abundant water, or social limits, such as desires for the maintenance of wild characteristics and Frontier characteristics in the landscape. Both proponents and opponents of Glen Canyon Dam, then, acted in response to differing

18. View north from northern edge of Page. The dark area on the upper right edge of the photo is the surface of Lake Powell. "Far beyond the dam, the reservoir . . . the town of Page . . . stretches the rosy desert. There is nothing to stay the eye from roving farther and farther. . . . Nothing grows out there but scattered clumps of blackbrush and cactus . . . a little scruf pea, a little snakeweed. Nothing more" (Abbey 1975).

mental images of the Interior West, and their pursuit of
these images has been to a large extent inscribed on the
landscape.

Just south of Glen Canyon, the settlement of Page grew
up on a formerly lonely, barren upland at the same time
that the concrete was being poured in the dam. Built to
support the construction at the dam site, Page today
serves as a tourist and service center for extreme northeastern Arizona. Seen from below the upland, near the
dam, its modern buildings of brick and stucco and wood
break the skyline with the angular forms of a Hopi pueblo
on a rock mesa. Page does not see itself, however, as a
modern version of a harmonious blend of culture and nature about which Indian spokespersons talk. In fact, Page
seems to have little sense of what it is. Although we
watched Navajos driving several old pickups and one
dusty car, and we observed Navajo men reclining on the
grass beneath a few small trees in the modest city park,
Page did not suggest its location in "Indian Country." The
buildings in a shopping center were trimmed in adobelike
stucco and adorned by Indian designs, and they were
grouped around a decorative "mission bell," an allusion to
early Spanish influence; but elsewhere in town no architecture or names reinforced either the Indian or the Hispanic images. In fact, the residential neighborhoods could
have been almost anywhere in a new, but not-too-elegant

suburb, as could the system for street names: trees on east-west streets and numbers on north-south streets. The names of businesses, moreover, were only mildly evocative of the specifics of the place—Desert Inn Motel, Page Boy Motel, Windy Mesa Lounge, Glen Canyon this and that. But maybe that is the image which Page wants, a new town built for a modern society. As a result it seems to be an anyplace town in a very special locale.

And what is the rightful place of the Navajos in this Anglo town? Their land was used to build Page, but the town was obviously not primarily for Indians or Indian needs. It is the sort of use of Indian lands that prompts progressives to cry "exploitation" or at least "insensitivity." Certainly, recent efforts by the Navajo people to gain greater control over the development of the natural resources, notably coal, on their reservations seems desirable, admirable, necessary, just, right. The greater prosperity to be gained through conventional economic development, however, is destined to mute the past and thus the traditional ways of life. The Turnerian progression may apply to cultures as well as to places.

For seventy or eighty miles beyond Glen Canyon Dam, u.s. 89 passes through an arid landscape of rock and sand, sagebrush and juniper, scattered grass, and still more scattered surface water. In places, high barren cliffs, typically tinged with red and brown and purple, rise up vertically, while elsewhere vast flat stone surfaces stretch endlessly beyond the horizon. The landscape seems too dry to offer much of utilitarian value to people: The Desert image continues. Even the crossing from Arizona to Utah is simply "somewhere" on this stretch.

Human settlements, new and old, have suffered in this desert landscape. About twenty miles north of the dam, the road bisects Glen Canyon City, conceived and promoted with high hopes several years ago as a "gold mine" for businesses to serve the boaters and fishermen flocking to the new reservoir. But the Big Rock Candy Mountain dream has faded away. If the community ever experienced a heyday, it must have been brief; open for business were only one tiny "grocery" store, offering gasoline for cars and "waterpuppies"—young salamanders—for bait, and a rock shop. Neither had a single customer. A gas station was closed down, and its overhang shielded the sun's rays from only pumpless concrete. Other deserted tourist facilities along the highway told of human hopes for the good life, lost to time and sun. Apparently, these lemonade stands were too far from the Playground.

19. Arizona-Utah state line between Page and Glen Canyon City. The south-facing cliffs of the High Plateaus region rise in the distance.

Farther along, a historical marker for the nineteenth-century town of Pahreah, a few miles off the road, told a similar history of growth and desertion. Here, though, the failure stemmed from an ironic but common problem of the desert—flash flooding. Although the humid regions of the country have a much higher flood potential, expressed as the probability of a flood of a given magnitude, than does the dry Interior West, the shallow soils, sparse vegetation, and steep slopes of arid mountain terrain produce rapid runoff of rainfall. Even modest precipitation, then, may suddenly fill desert stream courses with brown, boiling water.

For more than any length of u.s. 89, this stretch offered the fewest signs of human habitation. No planted shade trees, no flower gardens, no lawns, no driveways, no mailboxes, no English sparrows, no stray dogs; in short, no people or their usual trappings. Only a couple of range cattle, sluggish in the midday heat, lolled beside the road.

Twenty miles beyond Glen Canyon City, though, in all of this conventionally bleak environment, was evidence of the importance of this wild landscape as a resource. Beside the highway to the south was a small, new building, locked and unoccupied, and a sign announcing the way to the Paria (Piute for "elk water") Canyon Primitive Area, a

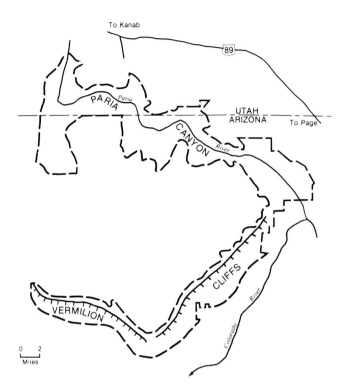

PARIA CANYON-VERMILION CLIFFS WILDERNESS. The 110,000-acre wilderness, established in 1984, is the largest on the public domain lands administered by the Bureau of Land Management. Along with the more well-known units of the national park and national wildlife refuge systems, state parks, and wilderness on the national forests, such wilderness areas on the public domain contribute to the protection of wild landscapes. As viewed by wilderness enthusiasts, these reserves are highly desirable; nonetheless, their creation as administrative entities helps to "fill" the landscape, to eliminate blank spots on the map, and "preserved wildness" becomes an oxymoron. (Map adapted from Bureau of Land Management 1987)

region of protected wilderness along the Paria River on lands administered by the federal Bureau of Land Management. This preserve was one of the first of two such protected wild landscapes to be designated by the Bureau in 1972; in 1984, it was included in an enlarged Paria Canyon-Vermilion Cliffs Wilderness, the largest unit of the National Wilderness System on lands administered by the BLM. This government agency, responsible for most of the publicly owned desert landscape of the arid and semiarid West, has become increasingly embroiled in controversy in recent years as it attempts to serve the needs of its publics for both commodities or energy and recreation or wilderness. The emergence of these pressures for establishment of wild landscape reserves in previously ignored landscape argues not only that the concern for wild nature has broadened to encompass hot, barren desert away from major river canyons, but also that the nation has become so crowded that even in such landscapes various groups vie with one another for influence. The Interior West, even outside its high mountains and its deep canyons, is today a landscape for a Protected Wild Nature.

Kanab to Montpelier

The first view of Kanab from U.S. 89 southeast of town was confirmation of what had been a hint, a suggestion, a whisper for the last several miles: The Desert, a persistent image since the ponderosa pine forest of Flagstaff almost two hundred miles back down the highway, was soon to disappear. True, one thousand feet of red cliffs still rose in the background; scanty sagebrush and rabbitbush still covered the slopes and lowlands; effusive heat still permeated the scene. But the line of trees running along the base of the cliffs at a right angle to the line of sight was a novelty. These trees marked not only the course of Kanab Creek, whose flowing waters washed aside the essence of a desert, but also the presence of a nucleated human settlement, the small town of Kanab, set within an otherwise wild landscape. Even the name "Kanab," from a Paiute word meaning "willow," often a tree of moist places, seemed to fit the new imagery. Here, as much as anywhere so far along U.S. 89, was the Middle Landscape, an agricultural Garden.

For the next two hundred and sixty miles of U.S. 89, as it climbs up the East Fork of the Virgin River, descends through the canyons and valleys of the Sevier River, and then rises up the San Pitch River in the Sanpete Valley, the highway continues within the Colorado Plateau region. But these are the High Plateaus, an area uplifted by faulting to produce a more moist, more forested, more verdant environment than the Colorado Plateau country farther south. The rivers fed by the winter snows of the highest elevations follow the faults, which are mostly aligned north and south. No less constrained are the cultural arteries—the roads also form a predominantly north-south pattern as they link the settlements in the river valleys.

Throughout this stretch of highway, the Garden image dominates the scene. Two dozen small towns are scattered along the way in the midst of hayfields and pastures, always with fields of brush or colorful cliffs or forested slopes or snow-streaked mountains rising above the agricultural lowlands. Mt. Carmel, Orderville, Glendale,

Hatch, Panguitch, Circleville, Richfield, Gunnison, Manti, Ephraim, Mt. Pleasant, Fairview—each resembles Kanab, established long enough ago to seem "old" today and with some exceptions, stable enough to remain economically viable without yielding to the temptations of the entrepreneurship that stimulates so much of modern growth. The details also consistently suggest the stereotyped small agricultural town—quiet main streets with stores housed in brick or stone buildings and offering "general merchandise"; modest homes with bordering white picket fences and front yards of marigolds, roses, sweet peas, and lilacs; back yards with tractors or hay balers, and sometimes with a few sheep or a couple of cows. A canopy of trees arching over the settlements shields them from the surrounding open, empty, and sometimes dry landscape.

Except for the details of housing, outbuildings and farm equipment, as well as the ever-present Mormon ward chapels built of stone or brick and over-topped by high, crossless steeples, these towns sometimes suggested to us the small settlements in the Upper Midwest. The feature that strongly reminded us that we were in Utah and not in Wisconsin, however, was the setting of wild landscape. In the Midwest, the woodlots or the open pastures always seem obviously humanized landscape elements, attractive to be sure, but long subjected to intensive human use. Here in southern and central Utah, wild nature seems stronger, and the landscape represents a more even balance of people and nature. If this were more often the culmination of Turnerian growth, the play would avoid the possible trappings of tragedy that it seems to many to have in Phoenix.

There is good reason why these towns evoke such a strong Middle Landscape image: They were planned and built with such a vision in mind. These are Mormon towns, and, in fact, they represent some of the earliest efforts by the Mormon Church to colonize its hinterland after the Saints first reached the shore of Great Salt Lake in 1847. From their initial settlement base, the Church leaders selected settlers and organized establishment of towns in the Sanpete Valley in the 1850s and in the drainage of the Sevier River the following decade. The towns, like all settlements of Mormon Utah, were designed to be homes for a chosen people to create an Eden on earth. The Mormons felt that they could create a perfect human existence, thereby redeeming the earth from the curse resulting from the sins of Adam and Eve. That sense of

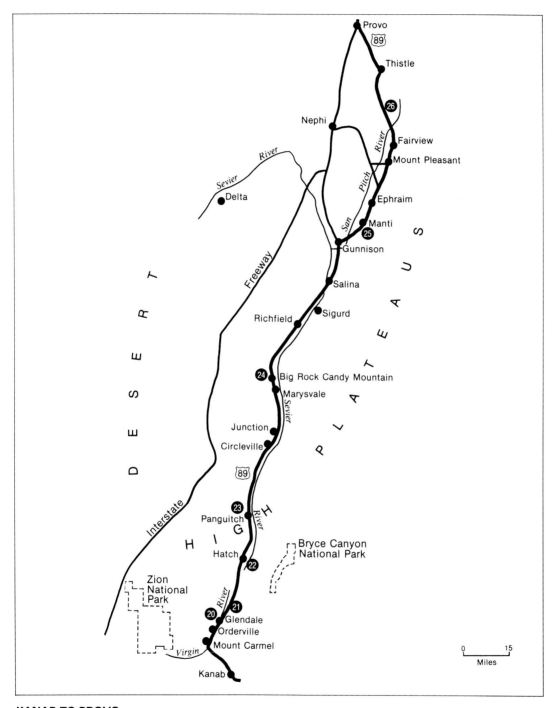

KANAB TO PROVO

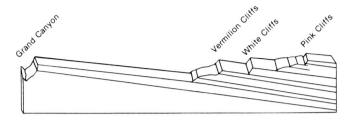

GRAND STAIRCASE. In the northern part of the Colorado Plateau, the stack of rock layers is tilted toward the north, and the erosional cliffs of the hard rocks face southward in the Grand Staircase. Kanab sits at the base of the Vermilion Cliffs, the same rock layer that is exposed in the Echo Cliffs. The valley of the Virgin River, where followed by U.S. 89, is bordered by the White Cliffs. The spectacular topographies of Bryce Canyon National Park and Cedar Breaks National Monument are cut in the Pink Cliffs.

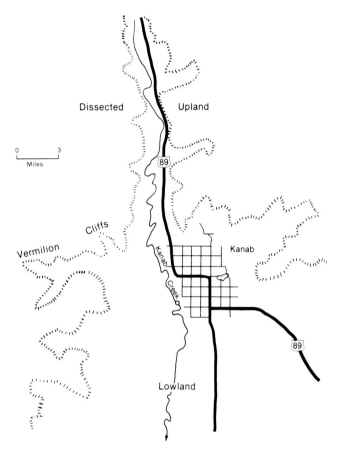

KANAB. The town of Kanab portrays the characteristics of the stereotyped Mormon settlement: It is set at the base of a mountainous upland, located beside a stream, and laid out in a rectangular pattern with wide streets running north-south and east-west; its blocks and lots are unusually large (Jackson and Layton 1976); it is small, strongly nucleated, with little fringing development.

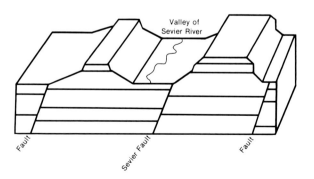

HIGH PLATEAUS. The valleys of the Sevier and San Pitch rivers are cut into the fractured rocks along the Sevier Fault. This section of the Colorado Plateau, called the High Plateaus region, is crossed by a series of such north-south trending faults, a structural feature that ties the area to the Basin and Range country just to the west. The uplifted plateaus reach elevations of more than 11,000 feet above sea level.

20. The town of Glendale, Utah. Shade trees hide most of the buildings in town, but junipers dot the gentle mountain slopes that rise above the settlement.

perfection was epitomized by the small, nucleated, self-sustaining agricultural settlement. Work with the opportunities that nature provides, the commandment said, but do not covet the misguided and cursed excesses in human society, and the resulting balance will provide redemption. Driven by "the militant hymn and sermon, not the smell of cash" (Snow 1988), the early Mormons tamed the mountain waters for irrigation in fields and pastures. These ideals were manifested physically in the landscape by the small Utah towns, Charles Peterson's (1977) description of which fits Kanab perfectly: "Almost all were laid out in the four-square pattern and were located at canyon openings according to the dictates of water and following the cardinal directions. They were promoted as the ideal form of settlement by the church."

The ideal of cooperation between people and nature, and among individual people within society, motivated the Mormon settlement of Utah generally but it particularly characterized the establishment of Orderville (aptly named), a few miles north of Kanab on u.s. 89. This town was initially settled in the mid-1870s when Church leaders, especially Brigham Young, felt that economic crises would be lessened and devotion to Church teachings enhanced if towns were established with a strong communal organization. "United Order" communities were formed and settled in this spirit, and Orderville succeeded as well as any from 1875 to about 1886 when economic difficulties and personal disillusionment ended the effort and property turned to private title. During its heyday, though, the citizens of Orderville ran cooperative farms and craft enterprises, pooled resulting incomes, and distributed earnings according to need. Whether or not it was a society freed of the curse which humanity has carried from the Garden of Eden is problematic, but Orderville still appeared symbolic of the balanced cooperation that seems part of the spirit of the Middle Landscape image.

The vision of a Garden dominates this stretch of U.S. 89, but the southernmost portion, notably around Kanab, also suggests the Cowboy West. Reportedly, Zane Grey, dean of the writers of popular westerns, lived in Kanab in 1912 while he was writing his famous (and anti-Mormon) *Riders of the Purple Sage* (Grey 1912). At the edge of town, a sign announces "Little Hollywood" in recognition of the use of the area for the filming of western movies in the 1940s and 1950s; another sign points the way to "movie ranch." The names on the stores along the business streets capitalize on this association between Kanab and the Frontier West and perhaps the Big Rock Candy Mountain part of the Frontier: Benny's Wigwam—Western Wear, Trail's End Restaurant, Gold Dust Cafe, Treasure Trail Motel. Both Spanish tile and adobe-style stucco embellish the buildings of the Coyote Cliffs shopping center. A stagecoach and a buckboard wagon sit outside Benny's; wagon wheels adorn fences, and verandas screen sidewalks; an eatery offers "Western cook-out" and a gift shop "sagebrush art."

The Frontier imagery continued north of Kanab. In Mt. Carmel, we passed the Mountain Man Trading Post, and in Glendale we admired the recently renovated but then-for-sale Smith Hotel, a good candidate for a western movie set. Across the street a new "old general store" enticed those eager for a bit of Western Americana. As we were leaving town, a dozen cattle, herded by a couple of young "cowboys," blocked our way on a side road, reminding us that the Old West is neither necessarily fiction nor entirely dead. Still farther north, in the community of Circleville, we encountered a western legend that blends both fiction and fact: Here was born Robert LeRoy Parker, a wayward Mormon youth who left his home and, as the better-known Butch Cassidy, according to Peterson, "robbed and charmed his way to a sure spot in the folklore of western badmen" (Peterson 1977).

This imagery of the Frontier West is likely promoted because summertime tourists yearn for an opportunity to be a part of that vision. Nevertheless, tourists also travel to southern Utah to enjoy firsthand the cliffs and canyons of Zion, Bryce, Cedar Breaks, Capitol Reef, Arches, Canyonlands, and Glen Canyon, which together with the Grand Canyon, comprise "a golden circle" of national parks. Although the asphalt of u.s. 89 nowhere extends into any of these parks, the route is a main gateway to these bastions of Protected Wild Nature. Most of the roadside tourist facilities, moreover, capitalize upon this interest in natural features and landscapes. At the Moqui Cave, complete with dinosaur, a sign warns drivers "Stop: Dinosaur Crossing" and promises "over 140 million years of natural history." Each town has its rock shops. Those at which we stopped were mostly quiet and empty of customers, even though the season was summer; a few people, like ourselves, were "just looking." No one of the shops was more intriguing in its attempt to appeal to the stimulus for the tourist trade, the natural landscape, than the building made in the form of a large rock with a waterfall plunging over its side.

In spite of these hints of the Frontier West and the Protected-Wild-Nature West, the dominant image along the highway in southern Utah was the Middle Landscape West. The high cliffs rising above the valley of the Virgin River, with its expanse of irrigated hay, typified this feeling. Pastures, thick with green grass and bordered by sagebrush, hosted cattle and sheep behind fences of woven wire and rough posts of juniper. Farther north, on the upper Sevier River, the town of Hatch had a main street even more rural than that of Kanab—a gas station, a grocery, a motel, and the ubiquitous rock shop, each hidden behind or set beside large trees; scattered homes, modest in appearance, were similarly sheltered beneath arching branches. Grandma Guent's offered leather goods and quilts. The side roads, more like rural lanes than town streets, provided access to homes more like farmsteads than town residences. A woman wearing a large sunbonnet worked her shovel in the irrigation ditch paralleling one side road; the horse in her front yard looked up as we drove slowly by, but she kept at her task of clearing the waterway at a deliberate pace. Nearby, an elderly man tended a small flock of sheep as they grazed the rank grass beside the road. We stopped at Quiley's, where we savored a lavish breakfast of tortillas, beans, chorizo eggs, and chili verde—all homemade. The friendly waitress, re-

21. Hay fields in the valley of the Virgin River. The bold White Cliffs rise in the distance.

22. Man with grazing sheep on a side street in Hatch, Utah.

**23. Main street of Panguitch, Utah.
The buildings are nearly a century old.**

sponding to our query, informed us that Hatch was not her hometown: "I'm from Arizona. My parents left me off on their way to California, and they're going to pick me up on their way back. I'll be here only a few weeks—that's the way it is around here." The Mormon ideal of stability persists in these towns, we suppose, but the American propensity for mobility cannot be entirely forestalled. The Big Rock Candy Mountain may be just over the next ridge.

Twenty miles down the Sevier River from Hatch, Panguitch (named for the Paiute words for "water" and "fish") was the first substantial community along U.S. 89 since Kanab. Multi-storied buildings of brick and rock standing shoulder-to-shoulder along the main street formed a true business district. The turn-of-the-century structures housed commerce for the farmer—auto parts and general merchandise—as well as for the tourist—Indian gifts and overnight lodging. Men in overalls and women in dresses lingered in pairs and small groups along the street, and these people who call Panguitch home outnumbered those who were passing through. Although the movie theater was closed and apparently abandoned, the town seemed to be economically stable—its surrounding fields, its operating businesses, its busy sidewalks all suggested Panguitch's continuing role as a viable agricultural service center. This sense of long stability in an agricultural town large enough to have a true business main street seems a necessary part of the ideal Garden image because it suggests the harmony between nature and human society that the image connotes. In turn, the stability of Panguitch is enhanced by both its persistence for more than a century and its lack of recent growth. No fringing K-Mart or Denny's, no enclosed shopping mall, not even a beckoning "Little Hollywood," mars the Middle Landscape of Panguitch.

A newspaper account of an ambitious, industrious, and successful entrepreneur of early twentieth-century southern Utah (Webb 1983) that we read while we were in Panguitch forced a questioning of the stereotyped Mormon pioneer, content with a lifestyle free from the materialistic pressures and goals of the non-Mormon world and thus a fitting resident of the Eden. Ninety-year-old E. J. Graff of Hurricane (named by a Mormon church official caught there in a storm), west of Kanab, according to *The Daily Spectrum* of St. George, had raised himself from a youth of poverty to an adult of means—"a millionaire several times over." Switching from teacher to storekeeper to chain-store manager to turkey farmer to egg producer to land buyer to cattle rancher, Graff kept "an eye to the future," expanding or changing economic activities when the monetary advantage prompted it. His is a life story that would please Horatio Alger as much as, or more than, Brigham Young.

Just north of Panguitch, the valley of the Sevier River opens up into a broad lowland several miles wide. The winter previous to our trip had been particularly wet, and the snowmelt had sent flood waters down to engulf fields and inundate roads; even when we passed by, in July, the Sevier River continued to boil with a high, muddy flow. Still, the scene was more pleasantly bucolic than threatening, and the numerous cattle grazing in pastures and the farmers working in hayfields and irrigation ditches seemed unaware of the nearby hazard of high water; if anything, the abundance of water, here and now at least, made the landscape seem more productive and the agricultural base more secure than it might appear in an average year. Only abandoned and deteriorating potato sheds detracted from the apparently healthy bucolic scene.

After passing through the narrow Circleville Canyon, the highway enters another broad valley bottom bordered by high mountains. Here was more enigma concerning the Garden image. The settlement of Junction was less prosperous than other towns farther south. Many small and old log houses were long-abandoned. Several newer, wooden homes were unpainted and in poor repair; a few were empty and apparently unused. Formal landscaping, generally sparse in the older yards in most of the earlier Utah towns, was here almost entirely lacking. In the yards, milk cows and sheep were more common than people. Still, a high school, seemingly new and well-maintained, bordered Junction on the north.

A few miles farther on, the town of Marysvale, named for the Virgin Mary by Catholic miners rather than the expected Mormon settlers, was even more symbolic of hard times; it was probably the most depressed human settlement along the entire length of u.s. 89. The main street was lined with mostly abandoned and boarded-up businesses—motels, cafes, general merchandise outlets, a visitor information center.

Both Junction and Marysvale were surrounded by seemingly prosperous and productive agricultural land, and thus in the midst of a pastoral ideal, there was evidence that not all was successful. Partly, the view suggested a theme common in rural America, in western America, and certainly in Utah—failure of marginal farms and depopulation of the agricultural landscape. But another factor, more insidious, may have contributed to the depression of Marysvale. The updated edition of the American Guide Series book on Utah reports that Marysvale enjoyed a boom from uranium mining in the 1950s and 1960s—a poignant expression of the Big Rock Candy Mountain—and that as a result "an abnormally large proportion of Marysvale uranium miners had died, or were expected to die, of lung cancer caused by radioactive radon gas" (Roylance 1982).

North of the town of Marysvale, the highway again hugs the Sevier River as it flows through the Marysvale Canyon, narrow and steep-sided except for a more open stretch that is home to the settlement called "Big Rock Candy Mountain." The mountain is a dissected mass of bare, yellow rock that rises for hundreds of feet above a gift shop, cafe, and rock shop. Unlike Marysvale, it seemed that human endeavors here have enjoyed success, success that befits the name of the place.

In the store, we found jars of "Rocky Minerals Water," allegedly "bottled directly from the 'Lemonade Springs' in the Big Rock Candy Mountain." A leaflet described its use as a drink and as an external treatment for "sunburn, burns, skin irritations, rash, cuts, wounds, sores, abra-

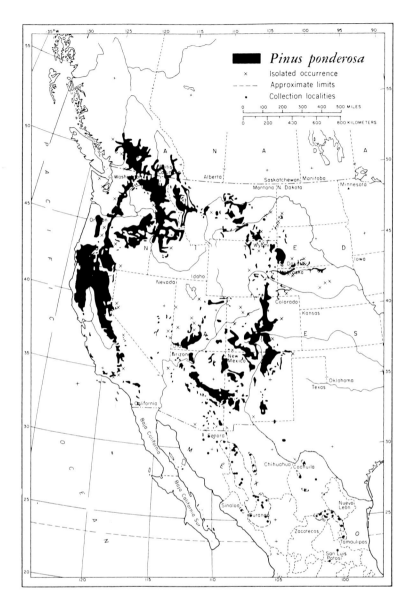

PONDEROSA PINE. Scattered ponderosa pine, also called western yellow pine, grows on the Big Rock Candy Mountain. Normally found at slightly higher elevations in this part of Utah, ponderosa pine succeeds here on the yellowish volcanic rocks altered chemically by hot water. Although isolated stands occur on such substrates elsewhere in the American West, ponderosa pine is not a tree restricted to unusual soils. It is familiar to residents and travelers alike as the most common and widespread tree in the mountainous West. For naturalist John Muir, ponderosa pine was also among the most appealing: "It is during cloudless wind-storms that these colossal pines are most impressively beautiful. Then they bow like willows ... glow as if every leaf were burnished silver ... [and] give forth the finest music to the ear" (Muir 1913). (Map from Critchfield and Little 1966)

sions, acne, blisters, etc." A second leaflet invited participation as a distributor of Rocky Minerals Water: "There is an immediate need for an additional 50,000 men and women in the [Rocky Minerals] industry. . . . The greatest expression of free enterprise in America. . . . No product in direct selling has a broader appeal. . . . No other product can compare. . . . No other business has a greater repeat potential." We pondered over which claim was more extravagant, the health benefits derived from using the water or the economic benefits of selling it.

24. Big Rock Candy Mountain, Utah. The resort beside the highway sits at the base of a mountain of yellowish rock which has been altered chemically by hot water. The trees are ponderosa pine.

The slopes of yellow rock are said to have inspired the folk song "The Big Rock Candy Mountains," written by Haywire Mac, a brakeman in the 1920s on the nearby Denver and Rio Grande Railroad. Alan Lomax (1960), in his *Folk Songs of North America*, reports that the author is Mac McClintock, teenage runaway, saloon singer, and railroad hobo. The original lyrics tell the story of a mythical Eden for hobos, a land "where the box cars are all empty . . . where the hand-outs grow on bushes . . . [where] the jails are made of tin . . . [where] there's a lake of stew and whiskey . . . where they boiled in oil the inventor of toil." Lomax indicates that "fifty years of reworking by other balladeers have obscured the raw irony of McClintock's original song, but have graced it with age-old Utopian fantasies," including lands where "men lived to be six hundred years old and finally died of laughter," or where "roofs were shingled with fritters steeped in honey," or where "roasted ducks flew through the air." McClintock may have earned some barroom coins with his song, but other singers, who reexpressed the Utopian sentiments and rereleased the song, probably made more substantial riches from The Big Rock Candy Mountains.

The resort, however, seemed not to be living up to its name. Few people were in the cafe; the motel was vacant; the rock shop was empty. We passed a "wild animal zoo"—a coyote in a too-small cage—on our way up a ravine to the Lemonade Springs, where lengths of plastic pipe were more conspicuous than the trickle of water. As we drove away, we noticed that the gasoline station and Hobo Mart across the highway were closed. Maybe our first impression of the success of the Big Rock Candy Mountain had been premature. Maybe the place remained a promise, a hope, and thus, some would say, more accurately represented the fantasy inherent in the Big Rock Candy Mountain image.

Beyond Big Rock Candy Mountain and the narrow walls of Marysvale Canyon, the Sevier River and U.S. 89 abruptly enter a broad, open valley of irrigated farmland bordered by mountains. Named for the richness of its soils, Richfield, the largest settlement since Flagstaff, retained a rural personality with pickup trucks and unpaved irrigation ditches, roses in gardens and sheep in yards, and a toiling citizenry in sunbonnets and overalls. In the Job Service office, few employment opportunities were available except for a country singer—"local preferred"; on the Safeway supermarket bulletin board, several ads offered piñon and cedar for firewood, goats for milk ("good milk line"), and a log cabin ("a pioneer relict") for a rental home. Still, Richfield was busier than the other Utah towns along U.S. 89 in the High Plateaus—more traffic, more traffic signals—and the Garden image was tarnished by signs of its defiler, the machine. A viable symbol of that industrial world, the railroad, had made a brief appearance in Marysvale Canyon, but here it was prominent along the highway. A string of coal cars, empty and quiet, sat on a siding, a reminder that Richfield is on the western edge of Utah's great coal region, an area which Peterson (1979b) contrasted with the Sevier River region: "Across the mountain to the east [the landscape] conforms much more naturally with the 'machine.' The railroad town, mining camp, and cosmopolitan population of the popular image suggest a harnessing of human and natural resources that goes beyond pastoral order to the productive discipline of the machine age." High voltage power lines, the first since Page, crossed the road north of town. At the nearby community of Sigurd, an unequivocal representative of industry was a plant of Georgia Pacific's Gypsum Division, complete with a stack disgorging billowing white smoke.

The highway continued northward through this com-promised Middle Landscape, through Salina with its live-stock auction and its coal companies, past lush pastures for the cattle and austere loading facilities for the coal, beside yellow-headed blackbirds flocking to the flooded fields and a lone drifter with boom box, stuff bag, and jacket trudging away from them.

Just west of Gunnison, the Sevier River was still brown and boiling in flood. Downstream seventy or eighty miles, the river disappears into irrigation canals near the town of Delta, at the edge of the still-empty desert farther west. Frequent water diversions along the Sevier River—some say that it is the most completely utilized river in Amer-ica—caused the Sevier Lake, beyond Delta, to dry up. (By the mid-1980s, unusually high runoff had refilled the lake, temporarily placing the Desert at bay.) The diverted water has been used to transform the Desert around Delta into an agricultural Garden. Recently, a coal-powered electric plant has carried this Middle Landscape, according to a local newspaper publisher, from the tranquil past into the troubled present. Citing a purse-snatching, an auto-theft, and numerous fights in bars, she expressed regret over the change wrought by industrial development: "It's been a caring community where people know each other and look out for each other. That's the way of life we chose by living here and that's what we're going to lose" (quoted by Omang 1981). The words of a cattle rancher who had sold his water rights to the coal plant, on the other hand, sug-gest disenchantment with nature's bounty in this Garden: "The land I was irrigating is pretty marginal anyway; never did make nothin' off it. The water rights were worth more than the whole damn place" (quoted by Omang 1981). The Delta farmer had tried to remain true to the yeoman's principles but had not reaped the promised har-vest of economic security.

In late June of 1983, the Garden character of Delta was more immediately disrupted by a force no less subtle than industrial development. The Sevier River, swollen with snowmelt, eroded and eventually broke through an earthen dam, sending floodwaters onto farmlands near Delta and forcing the evacuation of over one thousand people. Local news coverage showing residents struggling to minimize and then to repair the damage stressed the resilience of the Mormon spirit and gave evidence that Delta need not yet fear that it had lost its characteristic of the community members "look[ing] out for each other." Ironically, the greater threat was not the present tempo-

WESTERN BIRDS. *Many different bird species bespeak the American West—lark buntings on the plains of Wyoming, broad-tailed hum-mingbirds in the mountains of Col-orado, Brewer's sparrows in the sagebrush of Nevada, cactus wrens in the cholla and saguaro of Ari-zona. In Utah, the California gull is a special bird for the image makers of the West. A breeding bird on cer-tain large inland lakes of the Inte-rior West, including the Great Salt Lake (thus defying its common la-bel as a "sea" gull), the California gull allegedly saved Mormon grain crops in 1848 when large flocks swooped in to devour a plague of grasshoppers or "Mormon" crick-ets. Whether or not true, whether or not exaggerated, the story re-mains a healthy reminder, a strong metaphor, for the dependence of the human world upon the natural.*

rary abundance of water but, because of ruined irrigation structures, the later lack of it that would cause crops to suffer. In a Desert, moisture for human uses comes often to the wrong place, at the wrong time, in the wrong amounts.

Undependable supplies of water make western irrigated agriculture, whether on the Sevier or elsewhere, particularly vulnerable, its future uncertain. Exhaustion of ground water aquifers, accumulation of salts in fields, demand for scarce water by industries and cities—all make impossible an expansion of irrigated agriculture in the West, or even a maintenance of the status quo. In fact, the federal government's National Water Council report foresees a reduction in the acreage of irrigated cropland by the year 2000 (U.S. Water Resources Council 1978). And with that inevitable reduction will be a loss of ties between rural folk and a rural landscape: "My own home village of Orangeville [east of Gunnison, beyond the Wasatch Plateau] retired most of its hard-won farmland in a series of sales and transfers to Utah Power and Light. The water that brought agrarian dominion to Orange Seely's Saints . . . now runs up the cooling stacks of a pair of power plants nearby. All night long now, you can sit on the rooftop of my grandmother's outhouse and watch the strobe lights on the stacks illuminate the Valley with endless, eerie bursts of cadaverous light. It's as if God is taking a million nighttime snapshots of the abandoned lands for his Chosen" (Snow 1988). Delta and Orangeville portend the future of western agricultural water.

From Gunnison, U.S. 89 leaves the main Sevier River by turning abruptly to the east and then angles northeast into the Sanpete Valley, drained by the San Pitch River coming down from the north. In Manti, fourteen miles beyond Gunnison, the alternating threats of either too much or too little water were again obvious. Walls of earth and sandbags lined each side of a residential street to transform the roadway into a canal to carry snowmelt waters of a flooding stream safely through the town. In the spring of 1983, these temporary conduits had been common features in towns of central Utah, including Salt Lake City itself, but this was the only example still being used along U.S. 89 when we drove the highway that summer. Such trials were not new to the Mormons of Utah. Nearby Ephraim was flooded in 1908 when "seventy-five to one-hundred-ton" rocks rolled into town. In addition, cold and snow discouraged many other settlements— some were abandoned and then resettled—and it was only

25. This two-story brick house in Manti, Utah, is typically Mormon. The sandbags in the foreground create a flood-water channel within the street.

with persistence that the towns continued. Agricultural crops often failed in the early years, whether from flood, drought, or other hazard, forcing settlers to depend upon the Native American foods of thistle roots and lily bulbs. Mormons may have viewed such problems as a testing of their determination to create "God's Kingdom"; they certainly did not always experience their environment as a land of milk and honey, of ease and comfort, or even as benign. Perhaps, however, the creation of successful agricultural communities in spite of nature accentuates the Garden image because it stresses human agency as a positive and creative force in a world that was sometimes unkind and often unpredictable.

Manti otherwise seemed to be an ideal Middle Landscape. The fourth oldest community in Utah, Manti was established in 1849 as one of the first outposts of the initial Mormon settlement on the Great Salt Lake. Most of its buildings were brick, adobe brick, stucco over brick, and stone; their apparent great age and good condition suggested permanence and success. The business district was quiet. Lawns were more manicured than those farther south. The grounds of the Mormon Temple, and the handsome building itself, were neat and well-maintained. The fields and pastures and the turkey farm north of town seemed prosperous.

We explored Manti, Ephraim, and Mt. Pleasant on one afternoon before driving into the mountains to look for a campsite in the National Forest. There we found mud slides, flooded valley bottoms, and fields of snow (one resident from a town in the valley below, responding to our comment about the abundance of mountain snow remaining in early summer, had insightfully answered, "Yes, but most of it's downtown!"). The campgrounds were all buried under snow or swamped with water, so we retreated, with the sun already gone, to a motel room in Fairview. It was a circumstance that would allow us to experience an important character of the small towns of Garden Utah—isolation.

U.S. 89 north of Fairview had been closed months earlier by a massive landslide that buried not only a section of the highway and the adjacent railroad but also the town of Thistle. A large lake formed behind the slide, and all transportation along the route was abruptly halted. The major link between the Sanpete Valley and the urban centers along the Wasatch Front was cut, and the upper Sanpete Valley community of Fairview was particularly isolated. We were the only tourists, apparently the only "outsiders," in the single cafe of Fairview. While we ate dinner, a young family and an elderly couple "from up the road" also ate a meal; several men stopped to relax and talk "on their way home." All of the males were dressed in blue jeans, western shirts and belts, cowboy or work boots, and many wore straw hats. Their clothes were dirty with the mud of work in wet fields and ditches. Their talk was of alfalfa, high water, and truck repair. At breakfast the next morning, the scene was much the same, although the cafe was even more busy, this time with men on their way back into the mud and water. It was like watching musical chairs: As one finished his eggs and coffee, another would take his place. The conversations continued even as the participants changed because no two men left at the same time, and the topics were much the same as they had been the night before: depth of water and mud, cedar fence posts, railroad ties, and turkeys (referred to only as "birds"). During both meals no one looked at the newspapers sitting on the counter, and no one talked about international tensions or state politics or the outside world generally. We had noticed in many of these towns, in fact, that newspapers, even from Salt Lake City, were hard to find, that the books on world problems that we found in small libraries had been rarely checked out, and that television reception was typically restricted to two or three channels. Free of the responsibilities that took the residents to heavy tasks in the fields and farms, we had a pleasant, even relaxed, stay in Fairview, which seemed to be the sort of town that people often imagine when they picture an apparently quiet, bucolic existence.

26. Road closure north of Fairview,
Utah. The Thistle landslide is at the
base of snow-capped Spanish Fork
Peak, 10,192 feet high, in the background.

MORMON CULTURE REGION. As discussed by Meinig (1965), the sphere of
the Mormon Culture Region is the area
of the West in which the cultural traits
of Mormons are particularly important
or notable. These characteristics include such obvious features as high
proportions of Latter-Day Saint
Church membership and Mormon
churches, but also the landscape trait
of the small, nucleated agricultural
community and the demographic characteristic of a large family size. Much
of the Interior West seems rightfully to
be the land of Mormonism.

The isolation also seemed appropriate for the Mormon experience—the desire to be isolated from the rest of the country and the world was one of the primary reasons why the Mormon leaders brought their following to the mountain valleys and desert plains of Utah. This isolation was the means to escape the persecution that the Mormons had found in their earlier homes in Missouri and Illinois. Isolation was the condition that would allow the Mormon society to form their Eden on earth. Isolation was encouraged by church leaders as a means to protect their flock from contaminating influences of the non-Mormon world. Fairview, in 1983 a town cut off from its most direct route to Salt Lake City, seemed to epitomize this historical association between the isolation of Mormon small towns and their image as a Garden, a Middle Landscape.

North of Mapleton and Spanish Fork, U.S. 89 has left the mountains and mountain valleys and runs northward on the alluvial plain that borders the western base of the Wasatch Mountains. This elongated area where the Basin and Range region to the west meets the Rocky Mountains to the east is called the Wasatch Front. The north-south aligned fault blocks of the Basin and Range begin here and march off all the way to California; the high ridge of the Wasatch Range marks not only the easternmost ridge of that sequence but also the westernmost ridge of what are called the Middle Rocky Mountains. Rising abruptly over 11,000 feet above sea level and more than a mile above the lowlands of Utah and Great Salt Lakes, the Wasatch Range provides the water, the recreation, the magnificent setting, and the place-identifying imagery for the great urban area that sits along its western base.

Between Mapleton and Provo, the dominant landscape image continued to be a balance between human endeavors and natural phenomena. When we stopped to look at an irrigated orchard, we experienced a mixture of sights and sounds that reflected not only culture and nature but also the technology of the Turnerian modern age and the tranquility of the Garden: A domestic black cat slunk through the roadside grass, while a hawk circled overhead; a helmeted young driver maneuvered his three-wheeled recreational vehicle across the ruts in an open field, while a middle-aged man in cowboy hat and boots strode into a restaurant adjoining the orchard; a train whistled and a rooster crowed. Nearby, an expanse of duplexes and mobile homes rose beside a small cattle feedlot. Farther along, a freight train rumbled by the Pacific States Cast Iron Pipe Company while meadowlarks sang from adja-

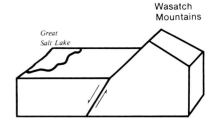

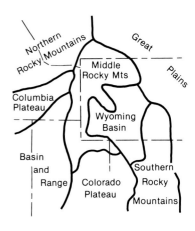

WASATCH MOUNTAINS. The Wasatch Mountains represent an upfaulted block, and the basin occupied by the Great Salt Lake is a downfaulted lowland. Such features typify the portion of the Middle Rocky Mountains in north-central Utah, an area that might be considered an extension of the block faulting of the adjacent Basin and Range region. Elsewhere in the Middle Rocky Mountains, the mountain structures also closely resemble the features of adjacent physiographic regions. The Yellowstone Plateau country, for example, is a northeastern extension of the volcanic activity that built the Columbia Plateau. The mountains in central Wyoming have resulted from broad upward archings of rock masses, which characterize the ranges of the Wyoming Basin and the Southern Rocky Mountains. Some of the mountains in extreme eastern Idaho echo the complex faulting of the northern Rocky Mountains. (Map adapted from Hunt 1976)

cent fields and swallows and gulls soared overhead.

From Provo northward, for about one hundred miles, U.S. 89 passes through the urbanized area along the Wasatch Front. At different times, the road is a freeway, a city street, a suburban highway, even a farm road. It passes through the distinctively named Mormon towns of Provo and Orem, Sandy and Murray, Bountiful and Brigham City, Ogden and Salt Lake City. In residential areas, the houses beside the pavement vary from the solid and well-maintained, multi-storied old brick homes of an earlier era (although gone are the logs and chinking of the Sanpete Valley) to the newer ranch-style houses of suburban America. Outside of residential neighborhoods, the road runs beside high-rise office buildings and long commercial strips, oil refineries, a steel mill, tar and chemical plants, and aggregate quarries, but also beside orchards with cherries, fields with grain and alfalfa, pastures with cattle and horses. The highway is wedged between the freshwater shore of Utah Lake and the salt water border of the Great Salt Lake (neither of which can be easily seen from the road) and the precipitous wall of the Wasatch range, always visible and always imposing, to the east. It is a route that is always busy with traffic.

In Provo, we stopped at the neat square of lawn and trees and flowers called Provo City Pioneer Park. Children laughed and romped in the playground; families picnicked on the grass; two solitary men in worn clothing slept peacefully on the benches; noisy gulls rummaged piece by piece through the litter in the garbage cans. A tall, slender monument honored the "Provo Pioneers of 1849" as well as the Mormon settlers who had died in the "Provo Indian Wars of 1850–1868." Nearby, four or five old log buildings had been moved to a plot protected by a chain link fence. Such reminders of the past were not unique, perhaps not even unusual, for a city in the West, but they seemed particularly appropriate where Mormons vividly perceive that their ancestors settled a desert and gradually developed a modern city. It is a Turnerian vision, here intertwined with Mormon religion and culture. More than anywhere else along U.S. 89, we sensed Turner's scenario of the West.

Twenty-five miles along this stretch of highway, beyond the cities of Provo and American Fork, we looked toward the west at the mountain of mine tailings at Bingham Canyon, conspicuously nestled on the flank of the Oquirrh Mountains about fifteen miles distant. We decided that we needed a closer look. Passing through the

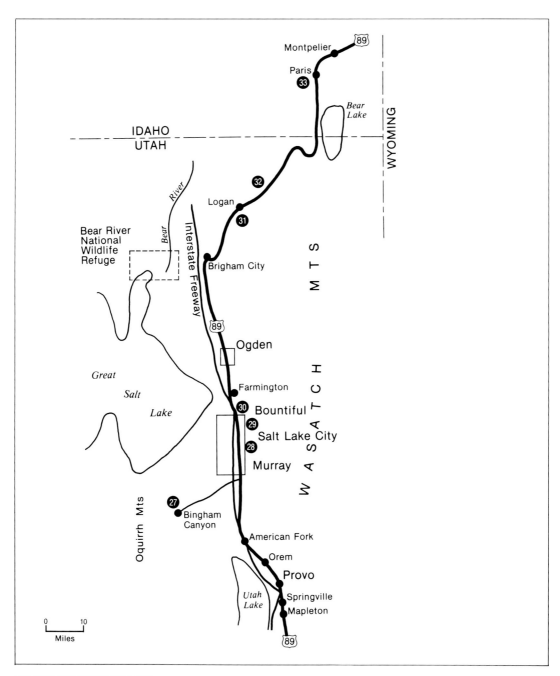

PROVO TO MONTPELIER

commercial and residential areas of Midvale and West Jordan, skirting the agricultural fields beyond the towns, and crossing the arid rangeland beyond the fields, the road rose gently toward Copperton, built and named by the Utah Copper Company and now a service center for the Bingham Canyon mine. The town was old, modest, and not-too-prosperous. The shade trees offered welcome relief from the desert sun, and the shopkeepers in the nearly empty copper souvenir shop offered a friendly welcome. The road beyond led into a mountain canyon lined by immense walls of golden yellow tailings and ended at a gate which, on that day, was closed to visitors. We could not view the world's largest open-pit copper mine. A congenial guard in a pickup truck, red light flashing, warned us away from scrambling up the steep slopes but otherwise encouraged us to view the scene and take pictures from along the road. As a vantage point for a photographer, the canyon floor was challenging. Westward, the looming tailings obscured the ten-thousand-foot-high mountain range beyond. To the east, however, we could see beyond the precipices of waste to the snow-capped Wasatch Range off in the distance, looking deceptively close in its frame of steel pipes and stacks of the ore-processing plant.

27. View westward in canyon of Oquirrh Range near Copperton, Utah. The railroad tracks, storage tank, and utility poles, all manifestations of industrial America, support the operations of the Bingham Canyon mine. Tailings from the mine rise to the left and in the background.

The distance between the mine and the settlements along the Wasatch Front may not be great enough for those who rue the intrusion of industrial society into the agricultural Eden. It probably would not be great enough for Brigham Young, who observed, in reference to mining, "Prosperity and riches blunt the feelings of man" (quoted by Sadler 1979). Other early Mormon leaders also distrusted mining because, according to historian Charles Peterson (1977), mining "would distort the balanced economy [with its] here-today, gone-tomorrow character." Although the mining for immediately useful ores like coal and iron was encouraged by the church, mining for precious metals like gold and silver was not. Moreover, even the extraction of approved minerals was considered desirable only for use within the Mormon empire lest it "would scatter the saints." Industrial development, especially mining, was a threat to the Middle Landscape of Mormon Utah, not only because such activity was antithetical to the Garden, but also because it invited diluting influences from the outside, gentile world. The Utah towns farther south on U.S. 89 suggested that, indeed, isolation was a critical factor in the Middle Landscape image.

Mormon fears over the heathen influences of mining were not unwarranted. In fact, the early United States government, concerned with discussion by church officials of an independent Mormon state, actually promoted mining in hopes that it "might deal death blows to both polygamy and church control of politics," according to Richard Sadler (1979). He suggests that the stationing of the 700 California volunteers near Salt Lake City in the 1860s, ostensibly to protect travelers and settlers from Indians, may have been designed to allow the military leaders, particularly Colonel Patrick Edward Connor, to explore for ore deposits and thereby encourage an influx of non-Mormon citizens seeking the Big Rock Candy Mountain. Perhaps not without coincidence, mining for gold, silver, and lead began in Bingham Canyon in the mid–1860s.

But even some early Mormons strayed from the antimining edicts of Brigham Young. In 1868, a group called the Godbeites openly broke from the Mormon leader and encouraged the development of gold and silver mines in Bingham Canyon, in the Wasatch, and in the deserts to the west; they felt that such wealth would increase the security of, rather than threaten, the Mormon empire. With the rise of the electrical industry in the outside world later in the century, demands for copper increased the importance of mining to the Salt Lake City area. As

Sadler (1979) comments, "By the turn of the century, Salt Lake City was surrounded by milling and mining towns and flush with mining money. With Brigham Young's anathemas forgotten, even Mormon men began to work side by side with immigrants in both the mines and mills." Brigham Young's fears had been realized: The "prosperity and riches" of successful mining in the Salt Lake Valley area had moved Salt Lake City forever beyond the agricultural base commonly regarded as both the Mormon ideal and the heart of our American character.

Certainly, growth has transformed the original Mormon settlement along much of the Wasatch Front into what seems to be the antithesis of the Middle Landscape. U.S. 89 through the core of this urbanized area—Salt Lake City and its adjacent towns of South Salt Lake, Murray, Midvale, and Sandy—forms a commercial strip fifteen miles long. Nothing like it borders the highway southward until Phoenix: fast-food outlets for the traveler and discount department stores for the resident; traffic that feeds the gluttonous auto and fuel industries; suburbanites rushing to jobs in the city and urbanites escaping to refuge in the suburbs and mountains. The smog here on winter days rivals the worst of Los Angeles in summer. This was not the Salt Lake City that an 1871 traveler had seen: "We came shortly upon the shore of the lake . . . . Smiling farms, neat small stations, white and brown cottages, children selling melons and milk, squared fields, English stacks, herds of cattle, trim fences, appeared as if by magic—a cheerful contrast to the wilderness through which we passed" (quoted by Rhodes-Jones 1979). That impression—that Eden—seemed now to be gone. Today, the difference between greater Salt Lake City and its rural and wild hinterland is even greater than in 1871, but the "contrast" seems not as "cheerful."

This perspective on what has happened to the Mormon landscape, however, is too simplistic. Although Brigham Young promoted the farm, he was not anti-urban. In fact, the nucleated gridiron settlement was encouraged as a means of maintaining the faith, encouraging the sense of human cooperation that went with it, and expressing, as Donald Meinig (1965) has described, "a rationally ordered society, a fitting frame for the New Jerusalem." The dispersed farmsteads that resulted from the heathen Homestead Act, in contrast, were considered inferior and undesirable. The pattern of concentrated settlement was part of the Mormon vision when the first Saints arrived in the Salt Lake Valley in 1847, so much so that Peterson (1979a)

has said that urban Utah existed before rural Utah.

The strong nucleation of people and power within Salt Lake City has allowed, ironically, the persistence of the Middle Landscape beyond the nucleus. Because of its centralized functions, Salt Lake City concentrated contacts with the outside world for all of the Mormon empire, and this concentration acted to insulate rural Utah from outside influences. As a result, the settlements in the hinterland have failed to reap the economic benefits and the economic growth that accrue to Salt Lake City; thus, towns like Fairview and Manti and Panguitch have maintained their less-cosmopolitan and less-prosperous Garden personalities.

From a vantage point in downtown Salt Lake City, on a low rise in what street signs identified as the "Capitol Hill Neighborhood," a few blocks from both the Utah State Capitol and the Mormon Temple, we looked down U.S. 89 toward the south. The snow-capped summit of the Wasatch rose prominently to the east, but in the foreground human artifacts dominated the long sweep of the urban scene. In our photo, Eagle Gate arches gracefully over the pavement two blocks away. It is a replica of the structure erected there in 1859 at what was then the entrance to Brigham Young's farm. A huge statue of an eagle still adorns the structure, but the farm, quintessential symbol of the Garden, was long ago consumed by Turnerian growth. The lone sandbag and several street barriers were reminders, however, that nature had recently expressed its continued strength here, as it had in other Utah towns, such as Manti, farther south along U.S. 89. Earlier in the spring, flooding City Creek was channeled down this street, State Street, and was dubbed the State Street River. Some locals so admired the rushing torrent, normally carried by an underground culvert, that they advocated a permanent surface stream. Two newspaper columnists expressed regret over the loss of the rushing water: "It's gone—we can't go out and take a look and see how it's doing each morning, lunch and evening. We can't see the tourists and the locals taking photographs of it with their Kodaks and Canons and Nikons. We can't watch the rocks rolling down, popping up. The coolness it brought with recently melted snow is gone. . . . The State Street River is now just a memory." The idea of a permanent surface stream, an intriguing vision that would have symbolized a closer balance between the human and nonhuman worlds, was dismissed by today's city fathers as "not practical" (Bingham and Linton 1983).

28. Commercial strip south of downtown Salt Lake City. The mountain ridge is part of the Wasatch Range, here rising more than a mile above the urban area.

29. View south on State Street, U.S. 89, from southern base of Capitol Hill in downtown Salt Lake City. The state capitol building is directly behind, and the Temple Square and Mormon Tabernacle are immediately to the right of the photographer's position.

North from downtown Salt Lake City, the Middle Landscape reappeared, although without the usual backdrop of
the small town. Instead, the scene was one of suburban
homes interspersed with rural vistas of cows and horses,
grain fields and orchards. Beyond these lowland features,
the mountain wall of the Wasatch rose abruptly. This sort
of landscape apparently is what historian Thomas Alexander (1979) envisioned when he commented that the
"best characterization of the Utah ideal seems to be suburban." Peterson (1979a), in quoting Earl Pomeroy, makes
the same point: "Much that was rural continued to be
manifest in both the Wasatch Front and in its two cities
. . . . The Mormons . . . 'brought rural ways into the city'
. . . [and there] continued to be a 'curiously rural quality'
to city life."

The visual impression may suggest such a balance between urban and rural, but some critics could say that the
prosperous suburban landscapes camouflage a sinister
economic base, a lack of anything close to harmonious.
Federal employment, especially in defense-related jobs, is
a strong component of the economy of the area north of
Salt Lake City, particularly in the Ogden area. Thomas Alexander (1979) has argued that "the decision to choose urban and industrial development over farming in the cases
of the Clearfield Naval Supply Depot and the earlier Ogden Army Depot (then Utah General Depot), built on
prime Marriott agricultural land, indicates the lack of
substantial agrarian sentiment in northern Utah by the
late thirties and early forties." The irony is twofold: Not
only is the Garden invaded, even displaced, by modern
technology of the highest and most destructive sort, but
also the independence and self-sufficiency that were part
of Brigham Young's Middle Landscape vision have been
displaced by reliance upon outside interests. Such dependence upon federal, and especially military, support is
hardly unique to Utah—it is a feature of the open spaces
of the Interior West and even the West more generally—
but it seems particularly surprising here, where nature
proffers an ample garden plot for the watering.

We spent a few hours at the Bear River National Wildlife Refuge, where the Bear River empties into the Great
Salt Lake, before we returned to Brigham City close to the
northern end of the stretch of cities and towns along the
western base of the Wasatch Mountains. From here, U.S.
89 turns sharply east, leaves the lowlands, and winds
gently into and through mountainous terrain before entering the lush Cache Valley, an idyllic scene of fields and

30. Horses and suburban neighborhood between Bountiful and Farming-
ton. The slope in the background is
the base of the Wasatch Range, here
spotted with clumps of Gambel Oak.

31. House and roadside canal, Logan,
Utah.

farmhouses enclosed by high mountains, topped by a few puffy cumulus clouds, and bathed in afternoon sun. At a roadside stand, we bought some raspberries—an appropriately fine and delicate specialty crop for this Eden—before driving the nine or ten miles across the valley to the town of Logan.

This mountain valley and town, like the Sanpete and Sevier areas to the south, were settled in the late 1850s and early 1860s as part of the initial spread of the Mormon empire from the western base of the Wasatch Range. Charles Peterson (1979a) has suggested that the isolation of Logan did not encourage Gentile immigration; this failure to "attract non-Mormons hampered [its] development and made [it] at once more Mormon and less urban than Salt Lake City and Ogden." Logan was laid out in the approved grid pattern and was situated, as had been so many Mormon towns along U.S. 89 since Kanab, along the base of a mountain range where a large stream leaves the mountains. The landscape of Logan, even with its Mormon Temple, however, did not look "more Mormon" than Salt Lake City or Ogden, except by virtue of the smaller size of the Cache Valley city. The residential neighborhoods were neat, well maintained, and seemingly prosperous, much like those along the Wasatch Front. There were no sheep or milk cows in front yards, as characterized the less elegant towns of central Utah, although many older homes were built of Mormon brick and stone. Newer ranch styles, less distinctively Mormon, with large shade trees and manicured lawns were also common. One particular home seemed to be a curious mixture of non-Mormon and Mormon traditions: a Cape Cod house, complete with dormers, fronting a streetside irrigation canal, strong symbol of early Mormon settlement. We wondered if Brigham Young would have worried about such an intrusion from the outside world.

From the eastern edge of town, beside the campus of Utah State University and at a high overlook which provides a fine vista over Logan, U.S. 89 enters the Bear River Mountains, still part of the Middle Rocky Mountains. At first, the highway follows the rushing Logan River in the deep Logan Canyon. The Playground image of this landscape seems apt: Ward Roylance's (1982) guide to Utah says that the Logan Canyon area supports "one of the greatest concentrations of [camping and picnicking sites] in the state . . . . Logan River is a popular fishery where German brown trout weighing more than 20 and 30 pounds have been caught. A maze of hiking trails and un-

OFF-ROAD VEHICLES. What the snowmobile is to the Great Lakes and New England states, the dune buggy and trail motorcycle are to the West. On the alpine tundra of southern Colorado, in the mountain canyons of Utah, or, especially, across the desert plains of southeastern California, motorized off-road vehicles are a common part of the recreational landscape. ORV's are despised by nature-protection environmentalists for their habitat-destroying, erosion-inducing, peace-shattering use, and some public lands are closed to off-road vehicle travel. The tension remains, however, vibrating between conflicting images of appropriate uses of the wild landscape as a Playground.

32. Boys fishing from a bridge in Logan Canyon. The lower mountain slope is forested with a mixture of conifers and broadleaf trees, with the conifers dominating at higher elevations.

paved forest roads criss-cross the mountains." In 1983, campgrounds provided recreational space for locals and long-distance travelers alike, including two who were taking pictures and writing a book. Many people were fishing in pools and quiet river stretches, including three boys on a campground bridge; no one was having much luck.

The forests and meadowy openings continue even after the canyon opens up onto a high, rolling upland, complete with a winter ski area and protected by Forest Service signs restricting off-road vehicles to established roads. Beyond the summit at almost eight thousand feet, the road drops steeply, leaves the forest in favor of sagebrush range, and enters the valley of Bear Lake, a lowland bounded by fault-lifted mountain ridges. The Playground image which had seemed strong through the mountains since Logan continued beside the famous light blue waters of the lake. Second homes were being built on the slopes, and tourist facilities were scattered along the southwestern shore. Bear Lake is known for its annual sport fishing for endemic Bonneville cisco, a kind of whitefish. It is an activity of winter, with either dip nets into the water or pole line through the ice, and we wondered if the winter cold could be as penetrating as the wintery blasts endured by ice fishers in the Upper Midwest.

Northward along the shore, U.S. 89 passes into the state of Idaho, and leaves the lake behind. In the small town of Paris, we wandered around on side roads, admired wooden buildings (notably uncharacteristic of the stereotypical brick masonry of Mormon towns) and photographed the famous Bear Lake Stake Tabernacle with a foreground of fields and a tractor and hay baler. Paris was settled in 1863, later than the Cache Valley, when Church leaders feared that the Homestead Act might encourage Gentiles and thus threaten the Mormon hold on the watershed of the Great Salt Lake. The winter cold in this six-thousand-foot valley nearly drove the Saints out, but they persisted and eventually succeeded, according to Peterson (1979c), in creating a small society where "people came as near [to] living up to the church's ideal of self-sufficiency as anywhere."

The handsome tabernacle was erected in the 1880s. A dance hall, complete with springs beneath the floor so that the surface would bound with the dancers, was built adjacent to the old building in 1913 but was torn down in 1979 because it "detracted" from the tabernacle. As was true for Indian ruins of Arizona, a certain purity is demanded in the preservation of old buildings, especially if

33. Paris, Idaho, with Bear Lake Tabernacle in background.

SAGEBRUSH. For the West, and especially for the Interior West, no plant seems to belong more than sagebrush. The name is commonly applied to any shrub in a dry western environment but more specifically to a particular member of the sunflower family, big sagebrush, *Artemisia tridentata*. A dominant plant in vegetation types of the northern Interior West, the range of the species extends north into Canada, east onto the Great Plains, and south into Baja California. It is scorned by livestock ranchers because it competes with the grass that fattens their cattle. It is looked upon with derision by impatient travelers who rush across the Interior West to get to the West Coast or the Rocky Mountains. But to anyone who has enjoyed the aroma of sagebrush after a summer thunderstorm, or admired the soft gray sweep of sagebrush in a lonely quiet valley, the plant remains a vital and appealing part of the Interior West. (Drawing of sagebrush from Sampson and Jespersen 1963; map adapted from West 1983)

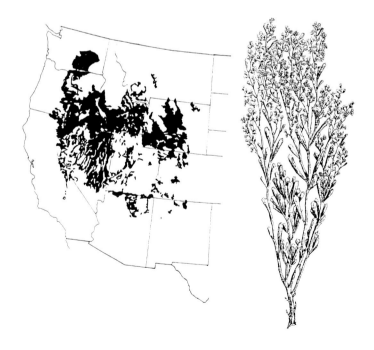

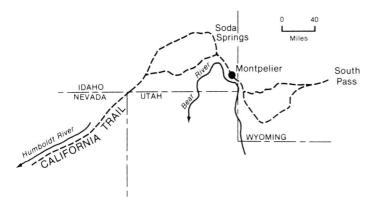

CALIFORNIA TRAIL/OREGON TRAIL.
U.S. 89 crosses the California Trail,
here synonymous with the Oregon
Trail, in Montpelier. Both north and
south of town, from the Idaho-
Wyoming border to just west of Soda
Springs, the trail closely followed the
present route of U.S. Highway 30, as it
runs along the Bear River's windings
between mountain ranges. For travelers along the old trail, this was a welcome segment of the route—watered,
wooded, level. The landscapes crossed
by the trail to the east and to the west
of this stretch, in contrast, were dry
and less hospitable. In the 1980s,
these more arid regions remain as
wild as in 1960, when author George
Stewart described them: "South Pass
itself remains an almost complete wilderness . . . in 1960 I drove . . . [on
what] was essentially nothing more
than the old trail itself. Except for my
companions, I saw no human
beings. . . . [The land from close to
Soda Springs] on to the Humboldt is
almost deserted, [and the primitive
road] still showed the characteristic
slight twistings and bendings which
result when oxen or mules break their
own way across country. One need not
be indulging in an impossible flight of
fancy to consider that these little
meanderings might go clear back to
[1843]." (Stewart 1962). Aridity, by
slowing natural change and discouraging human settlement, has allowed
persistence of a crucial vestige of the
Frontier West.

they are to be recorded on the National Register of Historic Places.

Ten miles beyond Paris, the highway passes through the
town of Montpelier, the largest town since Logan. A
bridge passes over the modern counterpart of the 1882 rail
line from Wyoming which had made Montpelier a ship-
ping point for the Bear Valley and which encouraged the
entry of non-Mormon influences from the outside world.
Even before the railroad, in fact, this locale saw non-
Mormon peoples passing through because it was situated
along the Overland Trail to Oregon and California. Perhaps as a result of these contacts, settlers in the Montpelier area were more ready to accept new ways, according
to Peterson (1979c). They adopted dry farming techniques,
for example, and introduced them to the Salt Lake area.
They depended less on surface water diverted in canals for
irrigation and instead saw the advantages of wells and
sprinklers. We did not sense this flexibility in the people
of Montpelier; instead we saw another attractive Mormon
town that represented the Middle Landscape. We did not
know that this would be the last such town that would so
unequivocally impress us on our travels north on u.s. 89.

Montpelier to Piegan

East of Montpelier, U.S. 89 leaves the drainage of the Bear River by climbing over mountainous country of trees and brush before passing from Idaho to Wyoming and dropping into the valley of the Salt River. Then, for about fifty miles, the highway heads due north within this level lowland called Star Valley, an elongated downfaulted block, before the Salt empties into the Snake River at Alpine Junction. This is high elevation farming country, full of pastures for livestock and fields of hay and grain; it is known especially for its dairy herds, and is home for the bulk of the Wyoming dairy farmers. The Salt River Range rises impressively to the east.

The Star Valley was settled by Mormons who trekked over the mountains from the Bear Valley in the 1880s and who considered it "the star of all valleys" (Urbanek 1974). After initial discouraging winters of snow, cold, and food shortages, they established a line of settlements, many of which persisted, but the rigors of the setting continued the hardships faced by the earliest residents. In 1927, eight one-hundred-pound tubs of cheese were hauled out during frigid winter weather, and nighttime fires were built to keep the cargo from freezing.

The area represents the northwestern edge of the contiguous Mormon culture region which spread out from Salt Lake City and through which U.S. 89 has been passing since entering Kanab in southern Utah. Unlike the small Mormon towns of Utah, however, the major town of the Star Valley, Afton, seemed to belong less to the Garden West than to the Cowboy West. The store fronts along the main street were mostly faced with wooden planks or shingles, instead of the more typically Mormon brick or rock; at least one building presented itself as a mountain chalet of European, probably Swiss, style. The arch built of elk antlers extending over the roadway seemed particularly suggestive of the untamed, untrammeled, and untrampled West—a region still wild enough to support the herds of great ungulates of a virgin continent. It matters little that the antlers come from the National Elk Refuge in Jackson Hole, not quite one-hundred highway miles to the north, or that the arch is painted with a protective coating of industrial-America plastic. The image is one of wildness, of a land still rich with the natural; even the explicit purpose of the antler arch, "to publicize Afton and all of Star Valley as a scenic part of the Old West, with its attractions of hunting, fishing, and camping," suggests this imagery. The story of the naming of the town also seems to fit: An early Scottish Mormon official "watched the rapidly flowing waters of Swift Creek, on which Afton is located, and remarked that poet [Robert] Burns could not have sung 'Flow gently, Sweet Afton' about this turbulent stream [and the name was adopted]" (Urbanek 1974). We found ourselves caught up with the wild Frontier—gone was the yeoman farmer of the Mormon Garden.

Afton's attempt to associate itself with the Cowboy West typifies all of Wyoming. Perhaps no other state has tried as hard to clothe its image in the brimmed hat and leather chaps of the American cowboy. A recent book of the history of the state makes this point forcefully: "Other states can rightly claim to share in the making of the cowboy myth; but Wyoming became the place where the script of the myth was written, and it enthusiastically adopted the image, imprinted it on its license plates, named its university athletic teams after it, and proudly continues to call itself 'the cowboy state'" (Larson 1977).

On the northern edge of Afton, we stopped to photograph a lumber mill, the logs for which were stacked in great rows which ended beside the highway. A tractor operator was busy moving small piles of logs back to the mill. It was a typical scene in the moister regions of the Interior West, but how different may be the further connotations through the eyes of various onlookers. Some might view the lumber mill as representative of exploitation from outside economic interests, from corporations whose officers and stockholders live on the coasts, whereas the local workers may view themselves as toiling in their own Garden. Others might see the mill as representative of the abundant resources of the Interior West, a Big Rock Candy Mountain. However, statistics indicate that this latter view would be misguided. Logging in the Rocky Mountains does not contribute much to the timber industry of the United States as a whole; less than ten percent of the sawtimber produced in the country today comes from forests of the Rocky Mountain region, and that percentage is likely to decrease over the next several

OVERTHRUST FAULTS. The mountain ranges along the border of Wyoming and Idaho are characterized by overthrust faults, low angle faults above which great layers of older rock have moved eastward and overridden younger rock. These geologic features lend their name to the region of recent gas and oil exploration in this part of the Rocky Mountains, the "overthrust belt." As a geologic structure, the overthrust is typical of the Northern Rocky Mountains. Its appearance here in the Middle Rockies suggests a tiny part of the Northern Rocky Mountains emerging south of the piles of lava on the Snake River Plains, part of the Columbia Plateau.

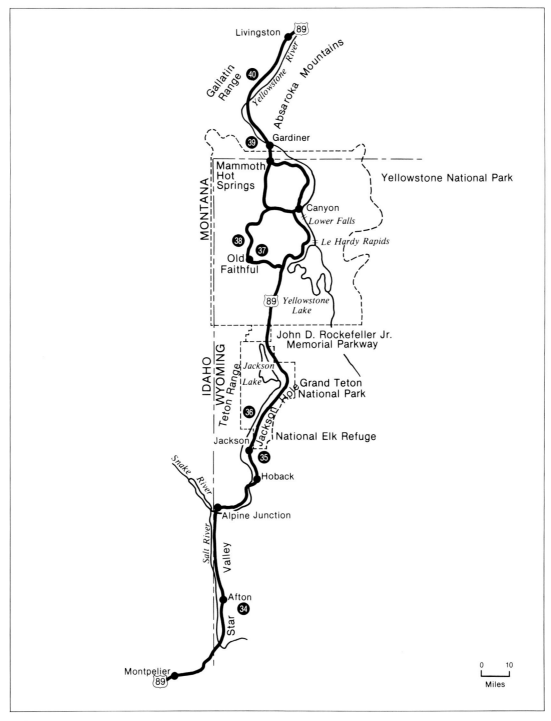

MONTPELIER TO LIVINGSTON

34. Main street, Afton, Wyoming. A sign identifies the World's Largest Elkhorn Arch.

decades. This more modest perspective on the timber supply of the region is paralleled by historian Dale Morgan's (1966) interpretation of the falsely fabled richness of Wyoming beaver before the arrival of the European fur traders: "Maybe the American West was rich only in poor man's terms." Poor folk marvel at the bounty of the wide, full mouth of the cornucopia, but after the feast they are dismayed by the scarcity in the horn's narrowing base. The image of the Big Rock Candy Mountain dies hard.

Farther north in the Star Valley, the same questioning of appropriate mental images, with much the same answers, was prompted by the sight of an oil derrick on a ridge overlooking a cache of baled hay. Here, certainly, was physical manifestation of several of our suggested images of the American West: At the bottom of the ridge rests feed for livestock, giving evidence of an extensive but modest economic activity characteristic of the Frontier or the Middle Landscape. But atop the ridge straddles oil drilling equipment that signals a Big Rock Candy Mountain vision of future intensive development of a rich resource base, which historically has fostered a Turnerian progression. The views of those wishing to preserve the Frontier or Middle Landscape, therefore, conflict with the views of those wishing to promote a Big Rock Candy Mountain image of this perceived Empty Quarter. Perhaps nowhere is the conflict of images stronger than here in the region of the northern Rocky Mountains commonly called the "overthrust belt."

Although contrasting perceptions of landscape meaning can be reduced only rarely to analysis of facts, this conflict, like the question of the timber resource, is addressed, in part, by objective inquiry. According to the Big Rock Candy Mountain vision, this is the region that is much publicized for its resources of petroleum and natural gas; its promoters claim that it can free America of OPEC blackmail. Nonetheless, the major reserves of oil and gas remain where production is already concentrated, in the big fields of the Gulf Coast and the plains of Oklahoma, in California and Alaska (National Petroleum Council 1972). These large deposits were found long ago, and the country has irreversibly peaked in its production of oil and gas, with no vast reserves left to be found. The notion of an untapped Big Rock Candy Mountain, still one more untapped and uncapped gusher over the next hill and beyond the fringe of the settled landscape, seems strongly implanted in the American mind. Our past has taught us that a rich wilderness awaits civilization, and we seem unable to accept the new lesson of modest, ultimately finite, resources. The Interior West has no vast reserves of oil and gas—it is rich only in "poor-man's terms."

After traveling beyond a reservoir and the recreational facilities at Alpine Junction, and passing through a deep canyon of the Snake River, U.S. 89 hurries beside scattered rural subdivisions before entering the crowded, bustling downtown of Jackson, Wyoming. No working Cowboy West is this—but rather a shimmering, scintillating, wild and rollicking Wild West show, it would seem, staged by the tourist industry to extract the gold and silver coins of "successful" American capitalists of the past generations, as well as the yuppies of the present. Today's dollars ride on the flanks not of cud-chewing steers but of two-legged tourists. One may easily envision ghost riders rounding up the crowds through the monumental elk-antler arches of the town square and herding them to curio shops offering Western paintings or "Indian crafts," clothing stores featuring the latest in "western wear," the wax museum pandering to the nostalgia for "old Wyoming," and a plethora of eating and drinking establishments promising chuckwagon fare: the Open Range Restaurant, the Wagon Wheel Restaurant, the Virginian Restaurant, the Elk Horn Restaurant; the Cowboy Bar, the Log Cabin Saloon, the Rancher Bar, the R-J Bar. Jackson offers all of this as well as a spectacular physical setting where nature provides long steep slopes for downhill skiing, a broad river for rafting, and open lands for horseback riding. Is Jackson the Frontier West or the Playground West? Or, here, does the Playground imitate the Frontier?

Almost from its beginning as a modern settlement, Jackson has appealed to those seeking the Cowboy West. In 1884, the first white settlers arrived in Jackson Hole ("hole" was an early fur trappers' word for a mountain valley, which they usually named for one of their group, as they did here at "Jackson's" Hole). About a decade later, a group of buildings became the locus for the town of Jackson. Farming mostly failed in the short growing seasons of the 6500-foot high valley, but small cattle operations provided a more viable economic base. The ranchers derived additional income, moreover, from guiding easterners and Europeans who came to Jackson Hole to hunt elk. In 1908, an idea spawned in Sheridan, Wyoming, grew and thrived in Jackson Hole—the dude ranch. Many working cattle operations expanded to provide for those city folk who wanted to "rough it" on less-than-elegant ranches, and dude-ranching became a way of life for Jackson Holers. One local of that time recalls that everything then was "based on horses and cattle and horseback-riding dudes. Everything—cabins, furniture, saddles, clothes—was indigenously Western. . . . Cattle was primary; tourism secondary. We still felt part of the Frontier" (Burt 1983).

The seeds of modern Jackson were sown early—the same local resident commented that even by the 1930s the town had become a center for "Nite-Life." But the expansion and diversification of tourism in the valley was a product of the post-World War II period and particularly of the last two decades. These recent times brought not only increased numbers of tourists operating on modest, family budgets but also, and perhaps more significantly, an influx of wealthy travelers whose contemporary tastes were less directly tied to the images of the Cowboy West than to those of the Playground West. Jackson has become a mecca for those who covet the golf course and tennis court, the sauna bath and racketball club, lounges and concerts, dinners with French wines and harp music—all while staying in luxurious inns or mountainside condos. We were impressed by the number of art galleries—one resident suggested to us that "every other store in Jackson is an art gallery of some kind"—and we were reminded of similarly wealthy Sedona in Arizona. Even the local free tabloid, the sort of advertising newspaper that is common in American towns, had a distinctive novelty that bespoke of Jackson's affluence—a page of Wall Street business

**35. Downtown Jackson, Wyoming.
The streets are busy with slow traffic,
characteristic of the summer season.
The swaths through the forest on the
slope in the background are ski runs.**

RIVERS OF THE INTERIOR WEST. The
three great rivers of the Interior West
begin close to each other in northwestern Wyoming. The tributaries to
the Missouri arc off toward the northeast and eventually sustain the Missis-
sippi. The Green River, major tributary
to the Colorado, heads due south. The
Snake River, feeding into the Columbia, swings to the northwest. Even the
eastern edge of the Great Basin, the
region from which no water reaches
an ocean, is nearby. Where U.S. 89 first
crosses the Snake, at Alpine Junction,
in a mountainous canyon close to the
river's source, the water flow is already nearly a quarter of the total flow
of the Colorado River. The Snake-
Columbia system carries a flow ten
times that of the Colorado, and the
Missouri-Mississippi system is more
than thirty times larger than the Colorado. The northern Rocky Mountains
and the Pacific Northwest are relatively wet, by western standards, but
the bulk of the West, most of the Interior West, is deservedly labeled as arid.
(Figure adapted from Hunt 1976)

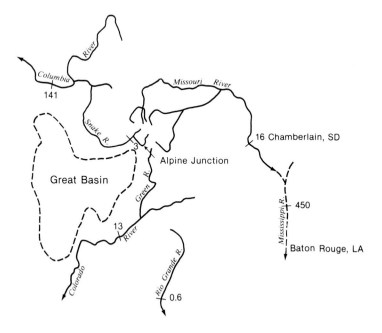

Numbers indicate average annual river flow in millions of acre feet

news and New York stock market quotations. (We thought back to the small towns of central Utah where we could not find a Salt Lake City newspaper on a regular basis.) The Cowboy West image of Jackson remains, but it is muted by economic prosperity and outside wealth.

Those who value, even cherish, the time when Jackson Hole was dominated by livestock operations and dude ranches regret what has happened to their valley. Even those who discovered the amenities of Jackson Hole and called it home before the most recent recreation and tourist development often despair about the loss of the rural atmosphere of the small mountain town. The same local who had "felt part of the Frontier" before World War II now finds things different: "Whereas in the past the contrast had been between Tenderfeet and Roughnecks, it [is] now between Natives and Tourists. Nobody much had used that Eastern summer-resort word 'native' to describe Jackson Holers in the old days" (Burt 1983). Today, however, the distinction is often made, and the dichotomy reflects a shift in what Jackson and Jackson Hole have become. "Tourism is king now; dude ranching and cattle ranching are secondary" (Burt 1983).

Ultimately, rural or wild landscapes and economic growth are incompatible. Whether or not the residents of Jackson Hole preserve a spacious Cowboy West or continue to develop their valley into a more crowded Playground West will depend upon what vision they have of their future and what meanings they see in their landscapes. It is a common dilemma that has occurred farther south on U.S. 89—in Tucson and Phoenix, in Sedona, perhaps in the Mormon settlements of Utah—where questions are being raised about the desirability of past, present, and future growth. The answers to these questions depend strongly upon the attitudes that people have about their relationships to the land, the meanings that they see in the landscapes that they are shaping. Some, though not all, meanings may be contradictory to others; the attempt to permit economic development in a directional, Frederick Jackson Turner West while maintaining a Cowboy West, or a Garden West, or a Wild Nature West will finally fail. In Jackson Hole, efforts to preserve rural landscape characteristics continue to focus equivocally on planning for growth, or regulating growth, or controlling growth, rather than decisively preventing or at least discouraging it.

The curtain across the melodrama swings closed abruptly and briefly at the edge of town for a change of

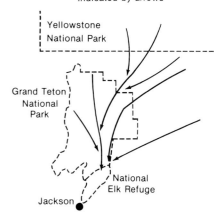

Major fall movements of elk indicated by arrows

Yellowstone National Park

Grand Teton National Park

National Elk Refuge

Jackson

ELK. American elk migrate down from the surrounding mountains to winter on the open vegetation of Jackson Hole. They congregate in unnaturally large numbers on the National Elk Refuge, where they paw through the snow to reach grasses and other herbaceous plants, but they also feed on baled hay provided by refuge personnel. Other valley bottoms are used by humans for agriculture—even in the sparsely settled region of the Interior West, both elk and humans covet the same landscapes, the same small areas which are moist and productive.

36. Visitors photographing entrance sign, Grand Teton National Park. The range in the background is the Teton Range, with Grand Teton at 13,766 feet high in the center. The flat area stretching away from the mountains and across the photo view is the sagebrush flat of Jackson Hole.

scenes. Immediately north of town, U.S. 89 runs below a steep ridge and enters the broad flat expanse of the heart of Jackson Hole. A high fence bordering the National Elk Refuge, which protects habitat for wintering elk, parallels the highway on the east for several miles before it yields to the entrance sign for Grand Teton National Park. Trophies are frequently collected here, but not of the elk-horn variety adorning the streets of Afton and Jackson. Here, as at entrance signs for most national parks, visitors vie to substantiate their success as travelers by clicking a shutter and capturing a three-by-five-inch glossy print of sign, relative, and mountain to mount in the family album.

The National Elk Refuge, administered by the U.S. Fish and Wildlife Service, and Grand Teton National Park, administered by the National Park Service, manifest the West as Protected Wild Nature. Preserving the land necessarily limits other uses. The open rangelands and wet bottomlands in Jackson Hole could be dedicated to unregulated livestock grazing, as they once were, but they are no longer. The Snake River could be dammed to provide storage for irrigation water for Idaho farmers downstream, as was proposed earlier in the century, but the dams were not built. The modest stands of aspen and pine, spruce and fir, could be harvested for wood products, but they remain uncut. The lakeshores and riverfronts might be lined by vacation homes, and the highways bordered by

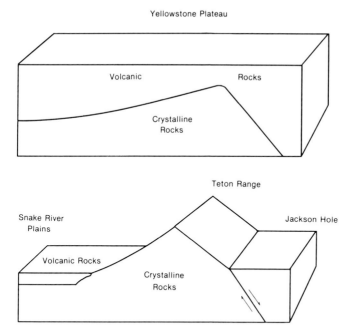

Yellowstone Plateau

Volcanic   Rocks

Crystalline
Rocks

Teton Range

Snake River
Plains

Jackson Hole

Volcanic Rocks

Crystalline
Rocks

TETON RANGE. The Teton Range is a block of old (more than 600 million years) crystalline rock uplifted strongly by faults along its eastern edge over the last several million years. Jackson Hole is an adjacent, downfaulted basin. The lava flows of the Snake River Plains, part of the Columbia Plateau region, border the Teton Range on the west. Northward, the crystalline rocks plunge beneath and are covered completely by the volcanic rocks of the Yellowstone Plateau.

motels and fast-food restaurants, but the landscape remains undeveloped. American society has dedicated the lands of Jackson Hole for protection of their wildness. The wild mountains, the wild river, the wild sagebrush range, and the wild elk are recognized as resources—not for the physical harvest or economic benefits that they might provide, but for their untamed character. The National Elk Refuge and Grand Teton National Park symbolize the perception and acceptance of wild nature as a resource.

Yet, to the residents of Jackson Hole at the time of park establishment, this use of wild nature as a resource seemed just one more example of the plunder of the Empty Quarter—even though the bounty was virgin land to be preserved in a park, rather than minerals, trees, or water to be exploited by outsiders. For more than two decades, between the late 1920s and early 1950s, John D. Rockefeller bought and maintained ranches totaling almost 34,000 acres in Jackson Hole with the intention of giving them to the federal government for an enlarged Grand Teton National Park (the original park preserved only the mountain range proper and little of the lowland of Jackson Hole). He was prompted to this act of philanthropy after visiting the area in 1926 and being urged to act by friend Horace Albright, whose career with the National Park Service is legendary. Rockefeller proceeded secretly for a couple of years, but when residents of Jackson Hole discovered that their ranches were being purchased by that most famous, East Coast, American aristocrat, they reacted strongly. Not only was an outsider buying up their lands, but also he was acting with the full knowledge and at least partial cooperation of a federal land agency, the National Park Service. Robert Righter (1982), in his history of the park, observes that the motivations of the residents reflected belief in a Frontier West: "For many, Jackson Hole represented one of the last bastions of individual freedom, and in some respects their attitude toward government control was not unlike their nineteenth-century frontier counterparts." Congressional investigations found no wrongdoing in the program of land purchases, but residents remained incensed and successfully delayed the transfer of the Rockefeller lands and the creation of the present enlarged national park until 1950.

Many of the residents resisted the park not only because it threatened their independence but also because they felt it might jeopardize their promotion of the area to tourists as the Frontier West. In the 1920s, some locals opposed formation of a national park but advocated instead a recreation area in which hunting, dude-ranching, and grazing could continue. Visitors could come, according to one account, to a "museum on the hoof—native wildlife, cattle, wranglers, all living for a brief time each summer the life of the early West" (Righter 1982). Righter suggests that even some early ardent supporters of the then-proposed park envisioned a continuation "of a number of guest ranches, thus retaining the flavor of 'the old West.' This flavor meant continuation of cattle grazing, often at the expense of competing wildlife." Many modern equivalents to the old dude ranches remain today and offer visitors opportunities to "live a legend of the Old West, . . . sleep under the stars or in [a] teepee tent, . . . ride through the mountain trails on Old Paint, . . . [enjoy an] Old West dinner, . . . look at the Jackson Hole backcountry as seen through the eyes of the Indians and trappers of yesterday, . . . leave [their] mark on the Old West." These sorts of activities are particularly popular in Jackson Hole and presumably attract people into the valley. Thus, Jackson Hole retains its image as a land of fur traders, even though no "rendezvous" was ever held there, and of cattle ranching, even though the operations have always been small and family-run, and of Indians, even though the most obvious reminders of Native Americans are exhibits in a Park Service museum.

Even for those who accept the Frontier West as a legitimate image for the wild nature reserve of Grand Teton National Park, other scenes of the Jackson Hole landscape within the park boundaries might seem less compatible with the national park ideal: The waters of Jackson Lake lap against a concrete and earth dam built in 1911 before the lake was added to the park; cattle graze where antelope roam; jetliners roar across the runways of a full-service airport within the park near its southern boundary; and, in the fall, as the aspen turn golden, sport hunters stream across meadows to "harvest" the "surplus" of the large migrating herds that cross park lands on their way to the National Elk Refuge. Moreover, Grand Teton National Park is not unique in such inconsistencies, some argue. Alfred Runte (1979) has suggested that the National Park System generally has enjoyed long and widespread success only because its units have been formed so as to minimize threats to conventional resource development; they are planned to avoid the areas most lucrative to the logger, miner, or dam-builder, but where boundaries overlap, wildness occasionally must be host to development.

No pure image alone, then, is adequate to explain American attitudes toward these western lands. Matthew Arnold once asked rhetorically of Victorian England whether Hellenism (emphasizing concern for beauty) or Hebraism (including reverence for work) was better for that country and concluded that both were needed; the question was one of balance. At Grand Teton, the scales are slowly tipping away from the Hebraism of despoiling our national resource of wildness in the pursuit of industry to the Hellenism of preserving it in the name of aesthetics: Livestock grazing will continue only for the lifetimes of the present ranchers and their immediate descendants, and not for just anyone with hungry cattle or sheep; proposals for additional dams have been rejected not only in Grand Teton but also in Kings Canyon, Glacier, and Grand Canyon National Parks. The airport and sport hunting remain exceptions, almost unique exceptions, among national parks and simply reflect the compromise befitting the long controversy that preceded the establishment of the enlarged Grand Teton National Park.

These images of the landscapes of the National Elk Refuge and Grand Teton National Park flickered through our minds during the days that we spent in the area. We thought about the appropriateness of the Jackson Lake

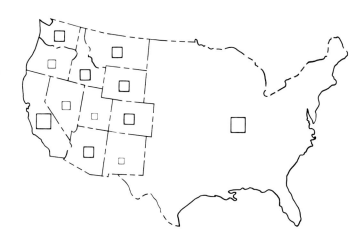

LANDSCAPES OF PROTECTED WILD NATURE. Of all the landscapes of Protected Wild Nature in the forty-eight states—lands in the National Park System, wilderness on the national forests and public domain, areas administered by the Fish and Wildlife Service, state parks—the bulk of the acreage is in the eleven Western states. The areas of lands of Protected Wild Nature are indicated by squares in each of the eleven western states and collectively for the remaining thirty-seven states.

Dam in a national park and were constantly reminded of the dam's existence by the drawdown ring of bleached rocks that identifies its shoreline as that of a human-made lake. (How many visitors, we wondered, recognize that the park's largest lake is a cultural feature?) We particularly fretted over the rebuilding of the seventy-year-old structure, perhaps with a higher reservoir level: Will this park continue to be a symbol of compromises that work against its primary purpose as a wild landscape reserve? We also tried to picture what the fall elk hunt must be like, and our minds went back to a television program that portrayed the hunters as over-eager predators, not necessarily skilled with their weapons, in a firing line for the slowly moving elk; the trophies so "earned" must be low in quality, Aldo Leopold might say. We looked around the historical features of the park, the Cunningham Cabin—where we learned about early ranching life—and Menor's Ferry—an early crossing of the Snake River—for example, and were tempted, unsuccessfully, to enjoy a "chuckwagon dinner" after a "trail ride." We wandered through the Jackson Lake Lodge, built by Rockefeller money and operated by the Grand Teton Lodge Company, itself owned by the Rockefeller family. Some observers feel that the building is too modern in design; others resent a lodge of any sort in a national park; still others resent this particular lodge's owner. We did not find ourselves objecting strongly on any score, as we admired the paintings and high ceiling of the sumptuous sitting room, encompassed by a magnificent backdrop of the Grand Tetons looming beyond a sixty-foot wall of glass.

Unquestionably, we were most impressed with the time that we spent enjoying the natural features whose preservation is the park's primary purpose. We walked through Blacktail Bottoms to enjoy the views of the mountains framed by stands of cottonwood and to look for ospreys and moose along the river. We drove the Rockefeller Parkway, where we admired the sweep of Jackson Hole abutting the awesome rise of the Tetons (alternately dubbed Tee-win-ot, or three pinnacles, by Indians; Pilot Knobs by the earliest Anglos; and Trois Tetons, or three teats, by the French trappers), searched the flats for pronghorn, and at one turnout joined a throng of bus-debarked tourists to offer handouts (illegally) to yellow-headed blackbirds.

The cynics poke fun at the American tourist in the national parks as someone deceived by a nature not quite natural, by a park not quite pure, and by motivations not quite honest. Such critics have a point, but often their cynicism is too general, too absolute, too unqualified. If there is continuing interest in Arnold's plea to stimulate "the care for sweetness and light, spontaneity of consciousness," if there is still validity in early preservationist Frederick Law Olmsted's claim that we create the parks to elevate the "contemplative faculty," there is unambiguous impetus to embrace our national parks.

North of Grand Teton National Park, U.S. 89 traverses a twenty-five-square-mile preserve designated as the John D. Rockefeller Memorial Parkway—created in 1972 in honor of the man who did so much for national parks. The highway runs beside the Snake River with a couple of tourist facilities for "river running" and camping. Then, it meets the southern boundary of Yellowstone National Park.

Yellowstone—this most famous of western, and American, national parks is mostly atop the great accumulation of volcanic rocks of the Yellowstone Plateau. Beginning about two million years ago, eruptions of viscous but more-or-less liquid lava and hot but more-or-less solid ash, the latter piling up before fusing together into hard rock, accumulated to build up the relatively level surface of the plateau. Rivers like the Yellowstone have dissected, in a few places, the volcanic rocks; glaciers have modified the stream-cut landscape; forests of lodgepole pine and Engelmann spruce sweep across the upland; winter snows pile deep upon its surface, a mile and a half above sea level. Still, the active geysers and other thermal features indicate that the volcanic activity is not over—either constructive eruptions of lava and ash that build up or de-

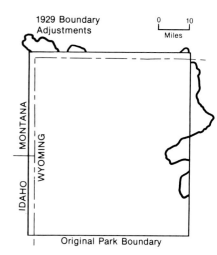

YELLOWSTONE NATIONAL PARK BOUNDARIES. The original boundaries of Yellowstone National Park enclosed a perfect rectangle, the sides of which were defined by a river junction and distances from lake shores. When established in 1872, the park was in an empty landscape: "No one knew what else was there; no competing demands existed; no one cared" (Luten in Vale 1986). After the turn of the century, Congress argued over revisions to the park boundaries, with park advocates particularly interested in a southward expansion to include the headwaters of the Yellowstone River and the Teton Range. The passionate and vituperative dialogue over these proposals suggests that the American landscape, even in the relatively wild Interior West, was already coveted by different people for different ends—

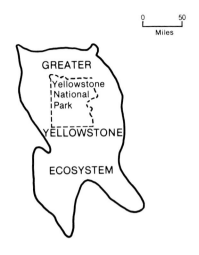

0   50
Miles

GREATER
Yellowstone
National
Park

YELLOWSTONE

ECOSYSTEM

people knew what was there; compe-
tition for land was growing; many
people cared: The landscape was no
longer empty. In 1929, in part to protect an area of petrified forest and in
part to redefine the park boundary
along watershed divides, modest
changes were approved by Congress
(Ise 1961). Even the most ambitious of
the earlier boundary adjustments for
Yellowstone pale in comparison to the
vision of the contemporary Greater
Yellowstone Ecosystem. This expansive area extends from Montpelier to
Livingston and from Cody to the Columbia Plateau. It is a region thought
by some to be necessary to protect
much of the natural integrity, whether
grizzly bears or thermal features, rein-
troduced wolves or continued forest
wilderness, of the Yellowstone region.

structive eruptions that lead to collapse of the Earth's surface could easily return. The mountainous terrain of the
West is fresh and new, active and alive.

Also full of life are the wildfires that occasionally rage
across the landscape of Yellowstone, as they did in the
summer of 1988. Ecologists have determined that fire
burned through the pine and spruce forests of the plateau
in pre-European times about once every two to four hundred years and that these fires characteristically destroyed
large areas of mature trees at one time (Romme and
Knight 1982). The great fires of 1988 were probably not
made hotter and larger by earlier fire suppression, simply
because wildfire had not been eliminated from the region
for a time sufficiently long to allow "unnatural" fuel accumulation. In addition, the let-burn policy, common today in parks and wilderness of the West and existent at
Yellowstone since 1972, cannot be easily blamed. Even
had the fires of this particular year been successfully sup-
pressed, there likely would have come another year, a
little hotter and a little drier, with the trees a little older
and perhaps a little sicker, when the fires could not have
been put out. Because of the apparent naturalness of the
fires of 1988, which burned parts of about one-half of the
park's forests, some ecologists are excited by the prospect
of the subsequent renewal: "It's not a big blast of fire—
[the burns are] mosaics, creeping around, torching up, laying down, creeping around again. . . . [Visitors] will see the
fireweed come in, and all the woodpeckers. . . . In another
year or two it's going to be glorious" (quoted in O'Gara
1988).

If the National Elk Refuge and Grand Teton National
Park represent and symbolize the West as a land of Protected Wild Nature, Yellowstone is one of the archetypes
for that image. Many people know that Yellowstone National Park, created in 1872, was the nation's and the
world's first national park, but many fewer realize that the
Yosemite Grant, designated in 1864, was the first wild
landscape reserve authorized by Congress but granted to
the state of California for administration. Regardless of
what area was first, however, no single feature is more
commonly recognized as a symbol for the national parks
than Yellowstone's Old Faithful Geyser; perhaps the
Lower Falls of the Yellowstone River would be its only
rival. About two million visitors come to Yellowstone
each year, and every single individual of those two million, it would seem, must wait to see Old Faithful erupt
at least once. Moreover, probably most walk to see the

37. Visitor waiting on boardwalk for eruption of Old Faithful Geyser, Yellowstone National Park. The heavy forest and gentle topography of the background are characteristic of the Yellowstone Plateau.

Lower Falls from a vantage point along the canyon rim; a surprising number walk down the short but steep trail to peer over the lip of the falls and get still another photographic trophy of their visit.

In contrast to the public lands to its south, Yellowstone's establishment unambiguously conforms to the image of the West as a land in which wild nature is protected as a resource. Yellowstone Lake is not dammed; broad meadows are not grazed by livestock; steam vents are not capped to generate electricity; elk and bear are not hunted; timber is not cut; curio shops and motels do not line the roads. Congress was not consciously setting aside a vast wilderness when it created the national park, but it was intentionally protecting from commercial development the singular scenic spectacles of Old Faithful, Mammoth Hot Springs, the Grand Canyon of the Yellowstone (whose yellowish rock walls befit the name "Yellowstone"), perhaps Yellowstone Lake, and various geyser basins. At the time no one knew what other geologic oddities might lie hidden in the thick forests of the Yellowstone plateaus, and, because no one much worried about locking up commodity resources in this area when a vast frontier remained undeveloped, Congress freely designated a large rectangular area of 3500 square miles as a wild landscape reserve. Only later would the park be valued as a block of wilderness as well.

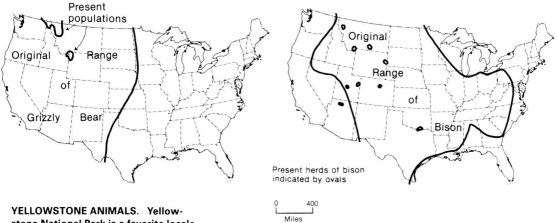

YELLOWSTONE ANIMALS. Yellowstone National Park is a favorite locale for visitors to observe large grazing mammals. Bison, elk, and moose are dependably visible. Much restricted from their former widespread ranges, bison and elk lend credibility to the image of the Interior West as the vestige of a virgin continent. Less conspicuous because of recent Park Service policies to discourage contact between bears and people, grizzly bears in Yellowstone are even stronger symbols of a wilderness West. (Information for maps from Burt 1976, Chapman and Feldhamer 1982, Schmidt and Gilbert 1978)

In addition to its preeminence as a symbol of Protected Wild Nature, Yellowstone suggests another image—that of the Cowboy West. Populations of wild ungulates, including mule deer, pronghorn, and mountain sheep, but especially small groups of bison and large herds of elk, not only impress visitors as features of wild nature but also remind them of a virgin continent, a Frontier past. They are viewed as evidence of nature's bounty before the advent of modern civilization.

Probably no wild animals have lured more visitors to Yellowstone than its famous (perhaps even legendary) bears—both black and grizzly, whose appeal early park administrators capitalized upon to increase park appreciation by promoting such Playground activities as bear-feeding sideshows. Unfortunately, the number of dangerous, even fatal, encounters between visitors and grizzlies have increased over the years as the bears have become less wary of humans as a threat and more dependent upon them as a source of free handouts. Moreover, begging roadside bears did not fit the natural image that the modern Park Service wanted to project, and its staff designed and implemented programs to discourage contact between people and bears. As a result, it is difficult today even to catch a fleeting glimpse of a bear through binoculars at one of the recommended overlooks, although they presumably remain unobserved in close proximity to those places which visitors frequent. Park Service policy, then, illustrates an effort to promulgate at least three views of the West at Yellowstone: First, bears must be returned to a more natural state, widespread and unthreatened by humans in their Protected Wild Nature habitat; secondly, the visitors must see the bears as free-roaming denizens of unfenced, unending expanses of Frontier-like territory; finally, and perhaps ironically, bears and people must be managed to avoid contact that would result in injuries that would tarnish the Playground image of the Park. Usually, the Park Service is successful at orchestrating these images to be compatible. But there are exceptions. In a recent year, an unwary tourist was fatally gored by a bison and a sleeping camper was dragged from his tent and killed by a grizzly just west of the park. Should such incidents increase, a choice among the goals, among the images, might have to be made.

Moreover, not all users of the surrounding area are either Park Service personnel or tourists, who embrace one or more of these three western images, so far assumed compatible. Rather, many are local ranchers or farmers who require a more tame stage of Turner's scenario within which to pursue their livelihoods, one in which bears as predators play no role except to be hunted and exterminated. One could even say that these locals see park preservation policies as exploitive, as though their lands were empty of uses contradictory to those of the Preserved Wild Landscape, the Frontier, the Playground. These contrasting views about what the West is or should be, what meanings western landscapes suggest or should suggest, continue to stir debate.

Other than through wildlife, direct links between Yellowstone and the Cowboy West are, compared to Jackson Hole, surprisingly limited. Only at the development called Roosevelt, in the northern part of the park, is the appeal to the Old West strong: "Board an authentic stagecoach . . . ride in a horse-drawn wagon . . . saddle up [and] take a trail to old-time adventure . . . enjoy [an] evening steak cookout." A sign for visitors leaving Roosevelt reads: "So long pardner—Come back soon." Also, the history of Yellowstone is prominent on the shelves of books and pamphlets in the park, and Old Faithful Inn has turn-of-the-century architecture, furnishings, and atmosphere—and offers a tour of the elegantly rustic old structure by personnel impersonating the chambermaids of a time long past.

The two national parks, Yellowstone and Grand Teton,

WARNING

NEARLY A DOZEN VISITORS HAVE BEEN GORED BY BUFFALO THIS SUMMER.

Bison can weigh 2000 pounds and can sprint at 30 mph, three times faster than you can run.

All animals in the park are wild, unpredictable and dangerous.

Stay in or near your car and do not approach wildlife.

YELLOWSTONE WILDLIFE LEAFLETS. National Park Service leaflets present the animals of Yellowstone as parts of Protected Wild Nature, but do visitors receive other clues, from characterizations of bears as "cute and friendly" or from recreational activities endorsed by the Park Service itself, suggesting that Yellowstone is a Playground? (Leaflets from National Park Service)

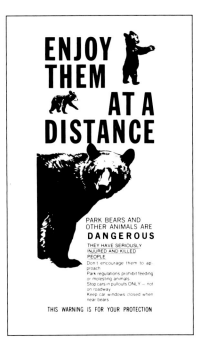

ENJOY THEM AT A DISTANCE

PARK BEARS AND
OTHER ANIMALS ARE
DANGEROUS
THEY HAVE SERIOUSLY
INJURED AND KILLED
PEOPLE
Don't encourage them to ap-
proach
Park regulations prohibit feeding
or molesting animals
Stop cars in pullouts ONLY — not
on roadway
Keep car windows closed when
near bears

THIS WARNING IS FOR YOUR PROTECTION

invite comparisons, we suppose, because they nearly ad-
join one another—what people choose to compare, moreover, reveals their perceptions of purposes of national
parks and thus of the validity of the image that they are
first and foremost wild landscape reserves. One such contrast, published in *The Denver Post*, was as amusing as it
was enlightening (Carlton 1983). Columnist Michael
Carlton disliked everything that he found in Yellowstone
as much as he admired everything in Grand Teton: "Yellowstone is a sideshow, an Edgar Allan Poe poem, a the-
atre of the absurd. The Grand Tetons are Broadway, a
Browning sonnet, a Shakespearean triumph." Among the
many park developments which he compared, Carlton
considered the restaurant meals to be of prime importance: In Yellowstone, he ate "ordinary food" and drank
"ordinary wine" whereas in Grand Teton he feasted on
"poached salmon, . . . roast loin of pork, and . . . a good
bottle of Sebastiani reserve cabernet." The nonedible
amenities of the meals seemed of equal importance to
Carlton: "[In] Grand Teton National Park . . . Polly and
Ester and Dennis the Menace give way to Prince Charles
and Princess Diana. These people actually dress up for
dinner at night, and I'm not talking about trading a pair of
white tennis shoes for a pair of blue tennis shoes. Some of
them even wear a coat and tie when they dine." Although
he admired a quiet herd of pronghorn in Jackson Hole, he
seemed less interested in national parks as wild nature reserves than as resorts, as Playgrounds.

We must admit that when we first visited Yellowstone
years ago, we shared some of Carlton's scorn for this earliest and heavily used national park. The crowds, the developments, the traffic, the congested campgrounds, the
forests of spindly lodgepole pines, the lack of high rugged
mountains all made that initial impression a negative one.
For us at that time, the most desirable of wild landscapes
would have had fewer noisy people and more majestic terrain. But with repeated visits, we searched out special
places and times that avoided the crush of humanity, and
we learned to savor the beauty of the many dramatic spots
which break the monotony of dense, even-sized timber
and gentle terrain. Mental impressions are strong—dawn
walks in the Upper Geyser Basin when the plumes of
steam are strongly backlit; nighttime eruptions of Old
Faithful when the sound of the forceful chugging of steam
and the light spattering of water on the apron of mineral
deposits are not compromised by the sense of sight; the
quiet but powerful gliding of the Firehole River in the

Lower Geyser Basin or the Yellowstone River below the Fishing Bridge—at times they seem the most beautiful waters in the world; the spotlighting of Yellowstone Falls from behind a thinning bank of clouds when a thunderstorm clears; a sandhill crane posing gracefully at the edge of a meadow and a coyote loping along a fringe of trees, each unnoticed by other visitors racing by in their cars on the nearby road; a small group of harlequin ducks bobbing lightly up and down on Le Hardy Rapids, hugging the shelter of the far shore, during a brief but heavy afternoon rain storm, while we watched from the dry cover of our car. These images of nature create for us an aura of magic about Yellowstone, a magic that many visitors must sense, that reflects our reverence for the wildness of that special place. Moreover, to our surprise, we have also come to treasure other, more cultural images which we initially regarded with some disdain. In particular, we now look forward to a yearly stay in the "old house" of Old Faithful Inn, immersed in the history of its rich Frontier past as we lounge beneath the three stories of an original lodgepole pine frame. But a common Playground for us it is not—and we laughed over breakfast as the little boy at the table next to us, impatient over Old Faithful Geyser's delay, anxiously peered through the window and queried his parents, "Is it broke?" We wondered how many adults, too, failed to appreciate the differences between the wonders of this natural world and the fantasy of Disney World.

38. Firehole River downstream from Old Faithful Geyser. The steam vents are part of the Midway Geyser Basin.

At the northern boundary of Yellowstone, just below Mammoth Hot Springs and just within the state of Montana, a special artifact is an attraction for the photography-conscious tourist—the old stone arch built in 1902 to honor Theodore Roosevelt. At the time, people traveled by train to Livingston and then up the Yellowstone River on a branch line; this was then the major entry point for the park, and appropriately for the times, the border was made more dramatic by the arch. The advent of automobiles has reduced the importance of this entrance and increased the use of those on the south and west, although even here short lines of autos back up at the border kiosk.

Beyond the stone arch, just past the boundary fence, is a view that represents well the use of landscapes inside parks as opposed to outside: a line of commercial establishments that was the town of Gardiner (named for an early trapper and mountain man). Equally impressive of that contrast in land use is the large herd of elk—a commercial game farm—that borders the highway on the far

39. Hitchhikers at northern boundary of Yellowstone National Park. The view is from within the park, in the foreground, to non-park land in the distance. The boundary extends from Roosevelt Memorial Arch on the left along the near side of the buildings of the town of Gardiner.

side of town. The sight of elk only twenty miles to the south and within Yellowstone usually results in a sudden braking of cars and a hurried rush out over the meadow for yet another photographic trophy. These game farm animals, in contrast, prompted no tourists to stop. Even the most urbanized of Americans seem to recognize the difference between wild and tame elk, at least when the latter are enclosed behind a tall fence.

Just downstream from Gardiner is the headquarters of the Church Universal and Triumphant (CUT), the Royal Teton Ranch. A refurbished, rambling, sky-blue ranch house serves as the major administrative building for the thirty thousand acres of Yellowstone River bottomlands and mountain slopes which presently support modular homes, a restaurant, and crops of carrots and potatoes; future plans call for additional housing and a school, cafeteria, and poultry processing plant. The Church moved from southern California to Paradise Valley on the Yellowstone River in 1981 and has been the subject of controversy ever since. Some locals distrust the Church's unorthodox ways; others resent the potential intrusion of as many as six hundred new residents in the Yellowstone River valley; some fear the loss of winter range for ungulates and habitat for grizzly bears; still others oppose the Church's plans to tap subterranean hot water, an action that could threaten thermal features in Yellowstone. Is it a domineering cult like that of Bhagwan Shree Rajneesh in Oregon, a murdering and suicidal group like that of Jim Jones in Guyana? Or is it a small and misunderstood religious sect whose leader desires simply a place to tend her flock? One point is clear: It is the largely wild environment that attracted the group to Montana. "The Book of Revelations in the Bible is going to be fulfilled," the Church leader predicts, "and the people and the planet are going to reap their karma in the form of plagues, diseases, economic problems and very possibly a nuclear attack by the Soviet Union. . . . The Royal Teton Ranch is where CUT is preparing to survive the spiritual holocaust" (Robbins 1987). The wilderness of the American West has often appealed to unpopular religious sects and to illegal or otherwise antisocial individuals and groups. The value that American society places on wild landscape today, however, means that the region can no longer be considered a refuge, a hideout, an empty place.

For the fifty miles below Gardiner, u.s. 89 follows the Yellowstone River northward, downstream, out of the mountains. The valley is mostly open and wide, with high

40. Valley of the Yellowstone River downstream from Yellowstone National Park. The mountains are part of the Absaroka Range.

peaks of the Absaroka Range climbing to ten and eleven thousand feet to the east and the Gallatin Range rising nearly as high to the west. The still broad and still majestic Yellowstone, now fringed by cottonwoods rather than pines, is here changing from a mountain to a plains river. This is ranching country of the Cowboy West, with vast pastures and irrigated hay fields, horses but surprisingly few cattle, and only scattered houses and outbuildings, some old and run down, but many others new and prosperous. Some well-known residents have reportedly included actor Peter Fonda and late author Richard Brautigan. Place names like Emigrant and Emigrant Gulch evoke images of the Frontier, as do the names of the businesses which cater to the tourists—the Old Saloon and the Livery Stable. Even a sign announcing riverfront land for sale has been erected by the L & L Land & Livestock company, rather than by some realtor identifiably from Livingston or Bozeman.

The land sales sign suggests that outside interests are eager to take advantage of the resources that mountainous Montana has to offer. As is true for travelers, the appeal of the Cowboy West is strong to potential homeowners. And, as is true in Jackson Hole, the locals may feel resentment toward such outsiders. The controversy over devel-

opment of Big Sky, a recreational and residential development in the Madison Range west of the Gallatins, attests
to such misgivings. Even stronger feelings are generated
by development concerns that want to use the waters of
the Yellowstone River, not for ranching and farming, but
as a source of cooling water for coal-fired electric generating plants. Worse still, in this vein, is the suggestion that
Yellowstone River water be exported to drier states to the
south or used to carry coal eastward in slurry pipelines. In
1978, the state reserved the Yellowstone River to in-chan-
nel uses, thereby protecting the wild character of the
stream, although the reservation rights are subject to pe-
riodic renewal. In addition, some locals may also resent as
an outside influence the existence of National Forest wilderness in mountains such as the Absaroka Range because
such wilderness excludes the land from local economic
pursuits, although Montanans are generally more support-
ive of such designations on lands within their borders
than are citizens in their sister states of Wyoming and
Utah to the south. Each of these functional uses, then,
connotes, for many Montanans, the role of Montana as a
land being exploited by other states, an Empty Quarter.

Beyond Livingston, established in 1882 as a railroad
town on the Northern Pacific, U.S. 89 leaves the Yellowstone River, which turns to the east and heads for the
Great Plains, and continues north by following the valley
of a tributary of the Yellowstone, the Shields River.
Twenty miles up this valley, small grain elevators emerge
above the gravel side streets and old stone buildings of
Wilsall, with the two-mile-high Crazy Mountains looming in the background. Here is an agricultural land that
does not suggest the Garden of Mormon Utah: The fields
of wheat are too large, and the homes are too few and too
widely scattered. There is no sense of the finer scale of
features in the Garden; absent are the intensively farmed
agricultural plots and the strongly nucleated towns with
shade trees and irrigation ditches. The juxtaposition of nature and culture is obvious, however, and maybe the vast
rangeland of brush and grass, usually visible beyond the
highway north of Livingston, emphasizes the natural
world at the expense of the human. As much as, or more
than, the Garden, this landscape seems to belong to the
sparsely settled, extensively utilized Frontier West.

This impression is reinforced repeatedly along the sev-
enty miles between Livingston and White Sulphur
Springs. The road is as sparse of traffic as any stretch of
U.S. 89; houses are fewer still. North of Wilsall, even the

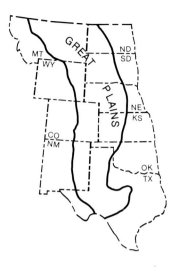

GREAT PLAINS. The Great Plains is an
elongated region bordered on the
west by the Rocky Mountains and on
the east, usually imperceptibly on the
ground, by the Central Lowlands. The
Great Plains may have little relief, but
its other characteristics seem to en-
capsulate many images of the Interior
West: It remains a Frontier of vast Indian land and even vaster livestock
range; for more than a century, it has
invited descriptions as either a pros-
pering wheat-filled Garden or a ruined
Dust-Bowl Desert; its strip mines harvest huge coal reserves of the Big
Rock Candy Mountain; its colonies of
ICBM's suggest the Empty Quarter; its
booming urban growth on the Rocky
Mountain Front epitomizes Turnerian
progress, in both its positive and negative connotations; its Black Hills support innumerable tourist attractions
and seem clearly a Playground. The
Great Plains also present an unusually
impressive visual scene, an American
scene, a Western scene: "Elsewhere
the sky is the roof of the world, but
here the earth was the floor of the sky.
The landscape one longed for when
one was far away, the thing all about
one, the world one actually lived in,
was the sky, the sky!" (Cather 1927).
(Map adapted from Hunt 1976)

MULE DEER. *The mule deer is the most common and widespread large mammal in the American West. Equally at home in coastal chaparral, mountain forest, alpine meadow, desert brush, or Great Plains grassland, the mule deer can almost everywhere find the grass and shrubs which are its primary foods. Like the coyote, the mule deer may be more numerous today than in pre-European times. It thrives in part because humans have inadvertently improved much of its habitat, by opening forest with logging and providing forage with irrigation, but also because public agencies monitor deer numbers and consciously manage to maintain high populations. The success of mule deer suggests that human activities need not always threaten wildlife species.*

wheat fields give way to sagebrush and grass and pasture, where occasional cattle and horses quietly graze. We did see four pronghorn and once noted several deer mingling with a small group of horses; a golden eagle soared high above the road in the summer heat. A single cow peered at us through barbed wire while crows perched on fence posts beyond. This sort of wild landscape has a special character to those who have settled and live in it. Writing in *The Solace of Open Spaces*, Gretel Ehrlich (1985) analyzes the impact that the vast open rangeland of the northern Interior West has upon its residents: "The dark side to the grandeur of these spaces is the small-mindedness that seals people in. Men become hermits; women go mad. Cabin fever explodes into suicides, or into grudges and lifelong family feuds." Yet, she finds a humane element to the endless space of such landscapes because it can connect as well as divide: "Space has a spiritual equivalent . . . and can heal what is divided and burdensome in us."

Ehrlich also alludes to the pioneer spirit that is still a requisite for habitation of this landscape: "People here still feel pride because they live in such a harsh place, part of the glamorous cowboy past." Her words, echoing off abandoned houses and barns scattered among the many still occupied and functioning, rang true to us. The apparent great age of the operating farms and ranches suggests the tenacity of people. This land's survivors are the Alexandras of Willa Cather's *O Pioneers!*, not the Berets of

41. Looking east down a gravel side street in Wilsall, Montana. In the distance rise the Crazy Mountains, named for their inhospitable steepness and "demoniac winds."

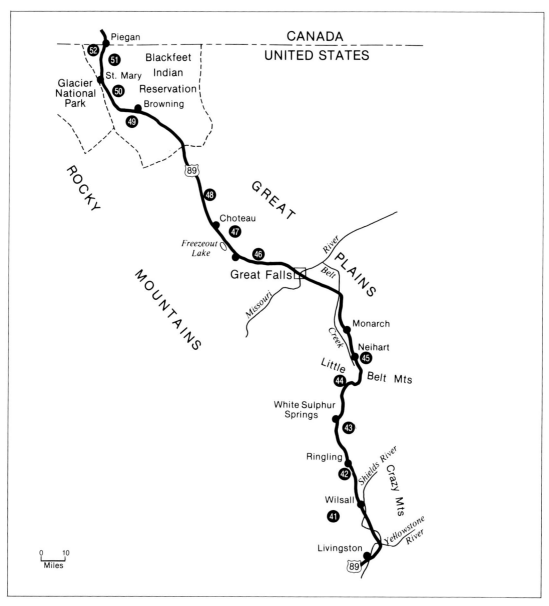

LIVINGSTON TO PIEGAN

O. E. Rolvaag's *Giants in the Earth*. It is appropriate that the film *Heartland*, a drama of the hard environment of the turn-of-the-century plains border and the quietly determined people who lived there, was filmed in these valleys. The Cowboy West, the Frontier, still seems strong here.

The next settlement, White Sulphur Springs, was named for the mineral deposits which rim the hot springs that were compared favorably by early resort owner James Brewer to the Baden Baden Spa in Germany (Cheney 1983). Today, the town is a ranching and sawmill town more devoid of tourist facilities than any town of comparable size along U.S. 89.

Beyond White Sulphur Springs, the highway climbs into the Little Belt Mountains, one of those isolated masses of mountains that dot the western plains of Montana. We camped in a Forest Service campground, empty when we arrived in the early evening—what a contrast to the crowded campgrounds of Yellowstone! Later, other visitors trickled in, including a couple from Germany. After donning swimming suits and cooling off for a few minutes in a deep pool in the cold stream nearby, they stopped to chat. They had come to the United States, rented a small camper—a Japanese model—and headed north on U.S. 89, the route of "all the national parks." They mildly complained about the crowds back down the road in "Yosemite"—an error in names that is as common among Americans as it apparently is among visitors from abroad. Regardless, they raved about the grand scenery in the parks—Zion, Bryce Canyon, Grand Teton, "Yosemite"— and they looked forward to the rugged peaks of Glacier. Their trip was reminiscent of a 1964 *National Geographic* trip along U.S. 89, then described as "the highway of the national parks" (Gray and Blair 1964). The appreciation of wild nature is not uniquely American; it is an old and persistent tradition in people. What narrow-mindedness it is to suggest, as some have done, that admiration of wild nature is an elitist and unhealthy trait!

The following morning, still within the Little Belt Mountains but near the Kings Hill Summit at 7400 feet, we stopped to photograph the clearcut forests of lodgepole pine. Even more strongly than the lumber mill at Afton, Wyoming, this sort of logged forest symbolizes for many the West as Empty Quarter, a land abused for products to be used by people in the East or on the West Coast. A Forest Service sign here assures the viewer that the clearcutting merely simulates or mimics the effects of fires in

42. U.S. 89 passing through rangeland between Livingston and White Sulphur Springs, Montana. The view is toward the south, with the Bridger Mountains in the distance.

43. Steer, old log barn, and Little Belt Mountains, just south of White Sulphur Springs. Dark forests cover the higher ridges, while range vegetation of grasses, forbs, and shrubs characterizes the lower slopes.

these forests, fires which naturally kill the trees and create large openings much like those produced by logging; a young forest establishes itself, the sign continues, on the resulting sunny slopes. Small trees are conspicuous here, although allegations had been made fifteen years earlier of abusive clear-cutting on the Bitterroot National Forest farther west in Montana. The issue of clear-cutting, like so many resource matters, is neither unambiguous in substance nor easy to resolve. Do critics of this logging also express outrage at the presence of seemingly natural meadows higher on the ridge above the clear-cutting? These openings may have been created by fire, perhaps set by American Indians or early Europeans—should the meadows be viewed as the product of deforestation, and therefore be seen as bad, or of ecological disturbance, and therefore be seen as good? The labels that are chosen reveal much about the perceptions and values of viewers, and thus of the meanings that are seen in the landscape.

44. Logged forest of lodgepole pine in the Little Belt Mountains. The area to the left is a clearcut, with young trees established on the open slope. The non-forested openings along the ridgetop are natural meadows.

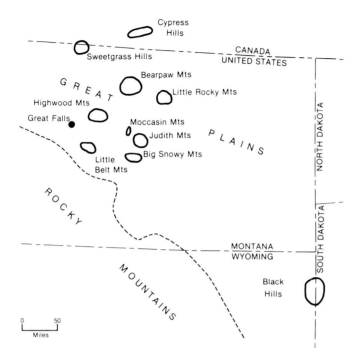

MOUNTAINS ON GREAT PLAINS.
East of Great Falls, gentle upward-
arching structures form small mountain ranges, blisters on the relatively
flat skin of the Great Plains. The Black
Hills are the largest and most well
known of these mountainous areas,
but those in Montana stand much
taller above sea level and above the
surrounding prairie. For the young boy
in Wallace Stegner's *Big Rock Candy
Mountain*, the distant Bearpaw Mountains seemed as mysterious and alluring as the western mountains,
whether in Montana or Colorado or
New Mexico, often appear to travelers
heading across the Great Plains, into
the great American West: "His eyes
turned into the low south sky, cloudless, almost colorless in the strong
light. Just above the brown line of the
horizon, faint as a watermark on pale
blue paper, was the tracery of the
mountains, tenuous and far-off...."
(Stegner 1943). (Map adapted from
Hunt 1976)

On the other side of its summit in the Little Belts, the
highway drops steeply down the valley of Belt Creek,
which drains northward to the Missouri River. A few
miles from the crest but well within the mountains is the
old silver-mining town of Neihart, named for one of the
prospectors who hit pay dirt here in 1881 (Cheney 1971).
Our first impression was that the settlement suggested a
one-time prosperity but a present-day stagnation. Behind
scattered cottonwoods along the main street sat low log
cabins among two-story upright homes with gingerbread
trim. Some were boarded up and apparently abandoned.
Others sporting Christmas tree lights and wreaths on
their porches on that warm July morning seemed to try to
hang on to better times, now past. A few houses were tiny,
and their backyard outhouses and stacks of fuel wood suggested that the modern world had not quite reached this
remote valley. Businesses were few—only one tavern and
a small grocery seemed to be functioning. A sign on a vacant lot announced the future home of The Prospector restaurant and motel, but who would be its customers? No
one was in sight. Like the road itself, Neihart was quiet
and empty.

We wandered around and discovered that our initial perception was not entirely correct. On the northwest side of the store, on a side street that paralleled both the highway and the creek, we found several new homes, elegant in their clean lines and smooth-sawn wooden walls, large rock chimneys and contemporary skylights, freshly poured concrete driveways and neatly manicured landscape plants. An elderly man appeared from down the street and from him we gained a different perception of Neihart.

The man explained that he had retired from a job in Great Falls, sixty miles to the north, and had built himself a cabin across the stream. He chose Neihart because "it has it all"—skiing, fishing, hunting, prospecting—and, besides, it is a "nice, quiet little town." Others, as well, had built summer or retirement homes here, he offered, but the trees hid them from view. A few tourists pass through in summer, and skiers come up from Great Falls in winter, but otherwise the town remains mostly unaltered by the outside world. Even its centennial celebration, held last year, generated only a little excitement. However, the reopening of the mine down the road, he thought, might stimulate more construction in town.

45. Old homes along main street of Neihart, Montana.

Neihart thus prompts a variety of landscape images. For the retiree, and others like him, it offers a Playground in a Garden, judging by what he chose to talk about. We doubted, in contrast, that our German friends, to whom we waved good-bye north of town, saw either recreational opportunities or Edenic qualities about Neihart. Old-timers might see the Cowboy West here, or perhaps, with the resumption of mining, the Big Rock Candy Mountain. Some outsiders might view the same mines as a modest representation of the Empty Quarter. No one image is right, and the others wrong. But we wondered if the elderly man's nice, quiet, little Playground and Garden would continue if too many people followed his example or if too much success was achieved, whether by locals or outsiders, in tapping into the Big Rock Candy Mountain.

Emerging from the Little Belts, u.s. 89 passes by fields of alfalfa and pasture on the edge of the Great Plains. It joins with u.s. 87, coming from the east, and then skirts around Great Falls, where it crosses the Missouri River, coming from the west and south. This most important city of the northern plains promotes itself as being "in the heart of big sky country" and offers, appropriate for the Frontier connotation of its promotional slogan, The C. M. Russell Museum. It also provides a hill-slope park overlooking the Missouri River and lines of grain-storage elevators; informational signs explain that Lewis and Clark portaged around rapids and waterfalls here, where the Missouri dropped four hundred feet in a series of five cascades, on their exploration west in 1805. Some businesses in the downtown have also invoked a Frontier image: Bonanza 88, Bighorn Wilderness Sports, Frontier Studio, Feedlot. Otherwise, though, Great Falls seemed hardly a town of the Cowboy West. Its multistoried brick buildings were more reminiscent of the contemporary heartland of mid-America, a Great Plains wheat and railroad town, than of the Frontier past. Consistent with the much-discussed plight of American farmers, some stores in the downtown were vacant (also a reflection of the closing of the zinc and copper processing plants over the last fifteen years), although newly planted street trees—we identified them as locusts—and pots of blooming petunias were signs of optimism, and the handsome elms in the residential neighborhoods (for which Great Falls is noted) suggested persistence. On the edge of town, a modern economic base was revealed by the Malmstrom Air Force Base, which a 1973 essay on Montana describes cheerfully as home to "200 nuclear-tipped Minutemen" (Peirce

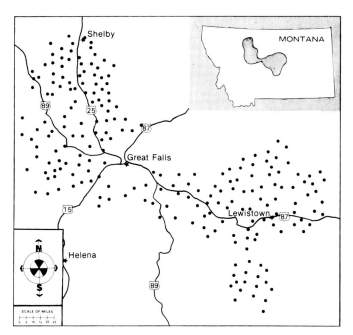

MISSILES OF MONTANA. The Great Plains around the city of Great Falls house a concentration of intercontinental missiles, testimony not only to its strategic location relative to the Soviet Union but also to its perceived utility as a landscape dedicated to national security. (Figure from Nukewatch)

Solid circles indicate missile silos

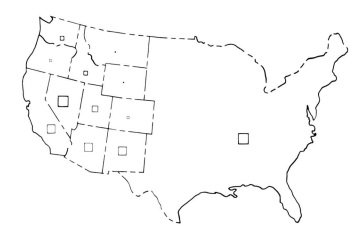

LANDS FOR DEFENSE. The bulk of federal lands dedicated to national defense—lands administered by the Department of Defense and the Nuclear Regulatory Commission—are in the eleven Western states. The areas of lands dedicated to national defense are indicated by squares in each of the eleven western states and collectively for the remaining thirty-seven states. (Data from Public Land Law Review Commission 1970)

1973). Another modern feature of the American city was the commercial strip along U.S. 89. The *Great Falls Tribune* featured a story on the new retail stores being built along the highway: a Dairy Queen restaurant, a new Kentucky Fried Chicken outlet, an appliance store, and a new "mini-showroom" for an auto dealer. C. M. Russell, Lewis and Clark, grain elevators, air force base, Kentucky Fried: Great Falls' claim to be the city that "best combines the worlds of west and east in Montana" seemed possible.

Beyond Great Falls, U.S. 89 heads to the north-northwest. It is now a highway of the plains. The mountain ranges of the northern Rockies are far to the west; although visible, they seem less prominent than the vast, rolling grasslands and occasional wheat fields which extend nearly to the horizon. A few houses, sometimes old log structures, sometimes new mobile homes, and usually modest and seemingly lacking in prosperity, were widely scattered. Meadowlarks, horned larks, and red-winged blackbirds were almost constant companions.

We stopped to talk with a friendly and talkative young man harvesting alfalfa hay with a new, massive, shiny, green, air-conditioned baler. In response to our curiosity about the great round bales that dotted the field, he explained that the large masses of hay store better in the fields—up to three years—than the more common smaller, rectangular bales, and they make economic sense on large ranches, such as the one where he was working. After glancing at our license plates, he asked tactfully, "Aren't farms in Wisconsin kind of small?" He then confessed that, for him, working a dairy farm was "too much work"; he preferred the hay ranch, where in the winter he was free, he said grinning, "to feed cattle, chase girls, and get drunk." (Having lived most of our lives in the year-round mild climate of California, we used to think that the snow-locked fields of Wisconsin winters provided that state's farmers with a labor-free season. But the Montana rancher was astute; dairy cows must be milked regardless of weather or season.) In a more serious vein, he lamented his government spending funds "to get us in a war" or loaning money "to other countries who would never pay it back"; instead, he suggested, the government ought to lend more support to its own country's farmers by helping them to avoid "buy-outs by doctors, lawyers, and attorneys": "Once you've lost the farms, you've lost it all." Then, abruptly, he went back to work. We watched him a while as the number of great circular green masses grew. We also admired the birds that he scared up, the ponds

46. Sky and grassland on Great Plains north of Great Falls, Montana. Low humidities in the American West produce the clear atmosphere against which towering cumulus clouds may be sharply etched. Both relatively dry climate and frequent burning probably combine to explain the treeless character of this environment.

that he drove beside, and the warmth and wind of his enviable world.

But what he may have perceived as an idyllic western life, a Cowboy West, a Garden West, was not what we read about in the local newspaper later that day or what we saw on the local television news that evening. Pesticide accumulations in grouse and pheasants have made them unfit to eat; water from the Missouri River might be sold to downstream states; grizzlies might be hunted in order to reduce their populations and thus decrease people-bear incidents; grain embargoes have hurt Montana wheat farmers; labor strife has continued to plague construction of a coal-powered electric generating plant and a natural gas pipeline. The images of an independent and self-sufficient West, whether as a Frontier or as an Eden, are illusionary. Yet the symbol is important. Even driving by as tourists, Americans can appreciate, however vicariously, their heritage of a close relationship between the individual and the land. And without these farmworkers' landscapes to arouse such sentiments, we agree with the hay-baler that one has indeed "lost it all."

At Fairfield, the "malting barley capital of the U.S.A.," the agricultural base seems healthy. Grain elevators line the railway siding, and the main street, running at a right angle to u.s. 89, is bordered by businesses for the working farmer. Names reflect the importance of agriculture, the Garden, rather than the Frontier or the Playground: Food and Farm, The Feed Store, Greenfield Farmers' Oil Company, Farmers Insurance. The high mountains of the northern Rockies rise far to the west, but the distance reduces their visual impact; the nearby low buttes with their short, rocky slopes and the vast expanse of rolling wheat and rangeland are more impressive.

Beyond Freezeout Lake (named for a group of soldiers who were caught unprepared by a blizzard), with its elusive flocks of ducks, and fifty miles northwest of Great Falls, is the small town of Choteau. This community has a special meaning to those interested in the American West: It is the childhood home of Western author A. B. Guthrie, author of a series of historical novels about the northern plains and mountains, including *The Big Sky* (1947) and *The Way West* (1949). In recent years, the town has become further famous for grizzlies that wander down from the mountains to the west and allegedly plague ranchers.

We were immediately surprised to see what Choteau was not. We had read a biographical sketch of Guthrie describing Choteau as a place "where he came to know and love the wide, wild, unspoiled grandeur of the high country." Choteau, at 3800 feet in elevation and with no appreciable relief except on the far horizon, is hardly the mountain town that one would expect from that description. (This misrepresentation, whether made consciously or subconsciously, is reminiscent of the Coors beer commercials which also imply an association with the Rocky Mountains, even though the beer is brewed on the edge of the Great Plains. The desire to be linked to mountains, wild and snow-capped, is strongly American.)

The Choteau that we found was another Great Plains wheat settlement (here, at the western edge of Montana's winter wheat region), with neat, tree-lined residential streets and a quiet business district; a line of tall grain elevators rose beside the railroad tracks and looked across the highway to the modest but sturdy Teton County Building. The town's structures did not reflect its great age (a post office and trading center were established here in 1775), nor its romantic namesake, Pierre Chouteau, once president of the American Fur Company, who

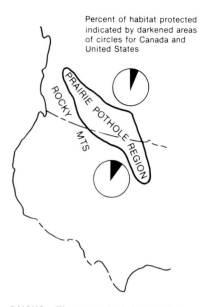

Percent of habitat protected indicated by darkened areas of circles for Canada and United States

DUCKS. The great duck factory for North America is the pothole country of the northern plains and prairies of the United States and Canada. Here in innumerable ponds and marshes are raised the family broods of mallards and teal, gadwalls and canvasbacks, baldpates and scaup which wing southward to the Gulf Coast and warmer environments each fall. Their wetland habitat is constantly threatened—sometimes by drought but always by agriculture. How this landscape is used—for ducks or for wheat—depends on the vision people have of the future. (Map adapted from Canadian Wildlife Service/Fish and Wildlife Service 1986)

47. Choteau, Montana. The grain storage structures to the right border the railroad, the Great Northern.

brought the first steamboat up the Missouri River (Cheney 1983). As we wandered the streets, we thought of Guthrie's book *Arfive* (1970), a story set in the fictitious town of Arfive, presumably modeled after his own hometown.

With *Arfive*, Guthrie's historical chronicle has progressed into the early twentieth century, and the town is changing from a ranching to a farming community. More generally, though, the saga of development and change for the whole series of books is encapsulated by the thoughts of a major character, Mort Ewing, who observes, on a westbound train, "landseekers" newly arrived from across the Atlantic. Ewing thinks that the newcomers expect so much wealth in the land that they anticipate seeing "dollars growing out of the ground. . . . All the poor bastards looking for Eden, looking beyond Norway, beyond Europe, beyond desk and counter, beyond east and midwest to full bellies and barns and glutted root cellars. And the only crop they could [really] count on was kids." The history of the American West, like the history of America, of the New World, tells of generations of people searching for the Big Rock Candy Mountain or the Garden but finding instead something far less toil- and worry-free. And the image persists today, we recalled, thinking back to the border fence at Nogales.

The pursuit of those dreams has continued relentlessly, with each new wave of landseekers changing the landscape in ways that bring regret to old-timers. Arfive's elder statesman feels "pulled in opposite directions" when he tries to accept the growth of farming in the former cattle country; yet, he seems to embrace a fatalistic view that suggests the West as a stage for Frederick Jackson Turner's drama: "In human numbers and enterprises this western country was growing and should be. Growth was health. Growth was foreordained, from seed to flower, from fetus to child to adult. And so it was with communities, from opportunity to exploitation, from cabin to village to city, from virgin soil to soil productive." We thought back to Phoenix, at the other end of U.S. 89, where we encountered similar sentiments about the inevitability of growth and change, and we recognized that the sentiment is strong in the American psyche. But are such characteristics really "foreordained"? Does continued growth make possible the achievement of a world that we will describe as desirable, of physical landscapes that will conform to our mental images of what we want as our habitat?

These types of concerns for the future arise in many regions, but in the northern Interior West, they are articulated in particularly thoughtful ways. The Northern Lights Research and Education Institute in Missoula, the Institute of the American West in Sun Valley, and the *High Country News* in Paonia, Colorado, are sources of ideas and opinions about the character of the Interior West, its society and its landscape. Each has expressed healthy skepticism about the pace and course of transformation of the region's land and human use of it, but each also has been wisely cautious about prescribing simple solutions. In a self-reflective essay on his newspaper's role in initiating desirable change, *High Country News* publisher Ed Marston recognizes that lasting change can only come from westerners, that "only the West can save the West": "The staff of *High Country News* is like a troup of ancient priests fingering the entrails of gutted birds in search of the future. . . . The stories in HCN can be almost as useful to the rural West as the birds were to ancient soothsayers. . . . Changing the values of the West's population, or the settlement of the region by people with different values, is a much harder job than going to Washington in search of a new law. Perhaps all we can do is accomplish what we can in Washington, as a stopgap, while we wait for the West to change at its roots" (Marston 1988). An ingredient necessary for the West to "change at its roots" is a vision of how it wants to change and how it wants its future landscape to appear.

About twenty miles north of Choteau, we found U.S. 89 passing through wheat fields laid out in the familiar zebra striping created by alternate strips of golden grain and summer fallow. The high wall of the northern Rockies rose in the hazy distance. It was hot and dry—the middle of a summer drought. Oil wells, pumping slowly in the sun, symbolized again the conflicts between the Frontier or the Garden and the Big Rock Candy Mountain or the Empty Quarter. Here, however, the conflict seemed subdued, almost insignificant—the wheat fields looked as productive where they had pumps as where they did not. The wells may even have added some attraction to the landscape. Is it possible that oil wells might be aesthetic assets, at least in certain situations? Like the power lines north of Flagstaff, these structures may satisfy a human need for "upright things" in horizontal landscapes. For America's early settlers of the prairies and plains, trees may have served as such geometric counterparts to the human form. Willa Cather (1918) voices these sentiments through the narrator in *My Antonia*: "Trees were so rare in that country, and they had to make such a hard fight to grow, that we used to feel anxious about them, and visit

48. Oil wells, wheat fields, and mountains of the Bob Marshall Wilderness, north of Choteau.

them as if they were persons. It must have been the scarcity of detail in that tawny landscape that made details so precious." For us, a comparable role was played by saguaro cacti in the deserts surrounding Phoenix. Perhaps the majesty that many see in grain elevators on the Great Plains may be similarly explained. For how many travelers do the nodding heads of these wells provide aesthetic appeal for the same reason?

Those answering in the negative would most certainly be those most enamored of a Protected Wild Nature image of the West, those like Wallace Stegner (1962b), who expressed delight to find himself "a challenging upright thing" in the wide, flat, empty stretches of his childhood prairie environment. Yet, Stegner today is hardly a recluse, braving daily the elements of some remote, uncivilized wilderness. Instead, he resides in the urbane society sprawling across the year-round green and tranquil hills south of San Francisco, more like the sheltered river bottoms that brought him "snugness" and "safety" as a youth than like the open grasslands whose rawness of wind, sun, and snow bred him strong and reflective. Perhaps a pure, single image of the ideal landscape even from an individual's perspective cannot be expected, or even necessarily desired.

Surely for all travelers the oil wells connote the human control behind the scenes. According to a recent history of the state (Spence 1978), "In Montana, the idea of colonialism, both as fact and myth, has been brought into sharper focus and has lingered longer than in most other states, in part because of isolation, but primarily because of the reality of the aptly named Anaconda Company," the great copper corporation that dominated the state for decades. "Perhaps only in Delaware, where DuPont was supreme, and in California, where the Southern Pacific maintained a stranglehold on railroading and politics . . . did corporate power compare with Anaconda at its prime in Montana." Suspicion about the beneficence of the copper king seemed justified when the mines closed, especially at Butte, although some continued to maintain that the state's economy generally had benefited greatly from the mining. Determined to cast off any role of victim and to guarantee their role of beneficiary, contemporary Montanans have placed constraints on mining with a 1972 addition to the state constitution that guarantees citizen rights to "a clean and healthful environment" and with a 1975 coal severance tax of 30 percent, highest in the nation.

Blue Grama

Little Bluestem

Western Wheatgrass

GREAT PLAINS GRASSLAND. The grassland along the eastern side of the Rocky Mountains is usually called a short-grass prairie. It is dominated by grasses of short stature, shallow roots, low productivity, and late summer dieback. By comparison with the tall-grass prairie in the more humid region farther east, the short-grass prairie seemed to early Europeans to be dry and desiccated—they called the area, along with the rest of the Interior West, "the Great American Desert." Some have argued that this perception is more illusory than real, and point to irrigation on the Great Plains. But irrigation is exhausting groundwater reservoirs; severe droughts will return, and blowing dust may again fill the air. (Drawings from Bureau of Land Management 1985)

The tax money may indeed be "the symbol of modern Montana," as a commentator has suggested; the state seems concerned with maintaining its images as Cowboy West, Protected Wild Nature West, and Garden West. A novel idea to save these landscapes within Montana is that of Robert Scott, who proposes a 15,000 square mile wildlife range (40 percent of the area of which is already owned by the public) in the "Big Open" of east-central Montana. Organized within a cooperative, "the land owner would be paid for allowing wildlife to feed on his land with hunting and guiding fees collected by the co-op. . . . Instead of 363,000 cows or sheep, there would be 320,000 wild animals" (Dawson 1987). Many ranchers are skeptical, but others recognize the economic security that such a plan promises: "They've done worse things out there—like farmin'!" Geographer Bret Wallach has suggested the same idea on a grander scale, a vast retirement of wheatland on the Great Plains from Oklahoma to Montana, a scheme of gradually paying farmers for their prairie restoration efforts until the land (except for small homesteads) has passed to federal ownership. "Established, the program will have enthusiastic support—and not only from environmentalists. . . . A sheep rancher from Rock Springs, Wyoming, said 'Christ, I love this country'" (Wallach 1985).

North of the oil wells, we stopped to exchange stares with cattle and horses that were seeking to cool off in a roadside waterhole on a hot afternoon. This was certainly the Cowboy West—range livestock, sparse vegetation, blustery and desiccated winds, dry and lonely landscape. The cattle in this empty location would have been potential targets of old-time rustlers, we thought, and judging from a newspaper article that we had read the previous evening, perhaps they are similarly threatened even today. The *Great Falls Tribune* (1983) reported, "The trade [cattle rustling] is flourishing in the New West, and it's increasingly sophisticated and profitable." High-speed trucks and interstate highways make possible the rapid movement of stolen livestock after "midnight fence jumping," although the major means of contemporary rustling involves a more modern and urbane convenience: Buying cattle with a bad check.

Twelve months after we passed through this area, wildfires raged across Montana's rangeland to the west, to the east, and to the south of this spot; when we read about the fires, we were reminded of our impressions about the Cowboy West on that August afternoon a year earlier. One

49. Retail store, old cars, and water
tower in Browning, Montana.

story reported that the year had been one "plagued by dis-
asters. First came the drought . . . then came the grasshoppers . . . the hailstorms, [and] in August, lightning."
The lightning bolts sparked fires that raced through western Montana and range fires that swept across the east.
"Our state is literally on fire," proclaimed the governor.
But one rancher whose land had been burned reacted with
optimism muted by fatalism—his was not unique determination, for the sentiment might come as much from a
victim of a Gulf Coast hurricane, or a midwestern tor-
nado, or a West Coast mudslide as from a burned-out
rancher in Montana. Yet, the words characterize the West
as a land that provides humans with a living only grudg-
ingly: "This kind of thing doesn't destroy people; it makes
'em strong. . . . You always hope that in the spring calf
prices will be better, the grass will be greener, and the
weather will be a little kinder. . . . You gotta start over and
count your blessings and hope for the best. This is kind of
next-year country, anyway" (Bassett 1985). This is not said
with bitterness—these farmers and ranchers are proud of
their Cowboy West. They certainly do not agree with the
view of their West as Desert wasteland as held by a traveling Wisconsin dairy farmer who told us (while we were
camped side-by-side in the Montana mountains) that he

would not trade his small Midwest farm for "one hundred farms on the Great Plains," and by the Illinois coal miner, now working in Montana, who allegedly said, "Mining is the best thing that could happen to eastern Montana. It's just a desert, anyway. Hell, strip it" (quoted by Spence 1978). But, then, such men were not born or bred in the harsh, open land that "mark[s] the sparrow's fall" and sadly lack the poetry and mysticism that Stegner attributes to its progeny.

For the next ninety miles, the last ninety miles of u.s. 89, the road crosses the one-and-one-half-million acre reservation of the Blackfeet Indians, named, some say, for their moccasins being blackened by the char of burned prairie. The Frontier image is conspicuous, although more for the open rangeland, here not converted to wheat or irrigated hay, than for tangible evidence of American Indians. Unlike the Navajo landscape, in which both frequent roadside jewelry stands and occasional sights of men or women in colorful dress remind travelers of whose land they are crossing, the Blackfeet landscape might be just more cattle country. Only in the town of Browning, headquarters for the Blackfeet, is there a conscious attempt to appeal to the tourist seeking "Indian Country." There, businesses such as the Warbonnet Lodge and Teepee Auto Parts seem less strident in imagery than a defunct, tepee-shaped cafe—cast in cement.

At St. Mary, thirty-two miles beyond Browning, the imagery of Native Americans was even more obscure. The small settlement offered tourist services for those headed to Glacier National Park, immediately to the west, but its buildings could have been anywhere in the Playground West. We ate pizza, for example, in a restaurant which displayed a license issued by the Blackfeet tribe; other than the clientele, nothing else suggested our presence in the land of the Blackfeet. Even the several motels and private campgrounds did not exploit the American Indian imagery fully; one campground advertised simply "Far-Out Camping," and although another was called Red Eagle, it compromised its cultural identity by proclaiming its membership in the Good Sam Club.

St. Mary also marks the westernmost point on a brief swing by u.s. 89 into the northern Rocky Mountains. From the plains around Browning, the highway heads due west and enters the rolling, partially forested, partially brushy foothills around Kiowa before it turns northward, climbs over a 5,800-foot high ridge, and drops down to St. Mary in the long, narrow, mountain valley of Lower St.

50. East wall of northern Rocky Mountains between Browning and St. Mary, Montana. The gentle, vegetated terrain in the foreground is within the Blackfeet Indian Reservation. The high, barren ridges in the background are within Glacier National Park.

Mary Lake. The roadway on this stretch is narrow and winding but, in the summer, teeming with tourist traffic of autos and campers and trailers. Homes, presumably of Blackfeet families, are scattered along the route, usually back in the trees or at the brushy edge of a meadow. Range cattle and horses often graze beside the pavement, and they sometimes surprise an unwary driver who rounds a bend and encounters three or four animals astride the yellow line, eyes fixed on the oncoming vehicle. The high, barren ridges in Glacier National Park rise to the west, but from the vantage points along the highway the mountain peaks appear more subdued than they do from the Going-to-the-Sun Road which crosses the park westward from St. Mary.

Beyond St. Mary, U.S. 89 proceeds northward, swings out of the mountains and back onto the plains. Twenty miles north of St. Mary, and three thousand miles north of Nogales, Arizona, at a few government buildings called Piegan, U.S. 89 reaches its northern terminus at the Canadian border.

This international line is in sharp contrast to the one at the southern end of U.S. 89. There is no bustling community, and little traffic. The two countries have, here at least, similar landscapes. A traveler would not be aware of

51. Looking west along gravel road and border fences at international border, Piegan, Montana.

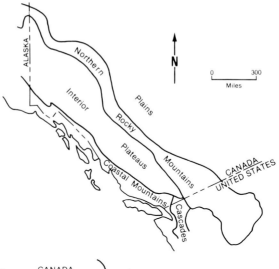

NORTHERN ROCKY MOUNTAINS.
The Northern Rocky Mountains are
characterized by spectacular thrust
faults, and the mountains in Glacier
National Park represent such over-
thrusts. As a geologic region, the
Northern Rockies of Montana and
Idaho extend northward into the great
continental wilderness of Canada and
Alaska. As a landscape, it is a region of
mountains and tundra, endless spruce
forests and undammed wild rivers,
bears and bighorns, wolves and wol-
verines. (Information for maps from
Dyson 1960 and Lobeck 1950)

the political discontinuity except for the signs that an-
nounce it. The fence is not recognizable as a border
fence—its only purpose seems to be to control livestock
like other fences back down the highway. Even the gravel
road paralleling the border might be just another farm
road.

Lacking is the rich Hispanic heritage which, along the
southern border, links the contemporary landscape to centuries of local history and even, perhaps, to the Europe
from which the United States originated. Instead, along
the border with Canada, the Frontier, the fresh, the new,
the future, is a dominant image. Chief Mountain stands
as the sentinel of the great wall of what we in the United
States call the Northern Rockies, but which in a larger
perspective is but the southern edge of the great continental Frontier which stretches from the mountains of Montana north through the virgin lands of rugged western
Canada and Alaska onto the vast, rolling Arctic tundra. In
looking westward, we sensed the sweeping arc northward
of new lands. Even the design of the multistoried U.S. border station, built of dark-stained logs chinked with white
plaster, seemed appropriate to the image, although the
less rustic appearance of the Canadian buildings suggested that our northern neighbors had some other image
in mind. Perhaps our initial impression of similarities
across borders was somewhat mistaken; as we observed
the line of northbound travelers awaiting interrogation by
the Canadian border guard, we wondered if he, like his
U.S. counterpart three thousand miles southward, envisioned himself as the guardian of a Big Rock Candy Mountain.

At this last stop of our journey, where we wandered
along the roadside just south of the border station, the
landscape to the south suggested two other visions, one
representing the United States as a whole. We saw before
us a recurrent vision of northern Montana: wheat fields
stretching to the mountains and the mountains stretching
to the sky. Our thinking took us to a familiar song: "O
beautiful for spacious skies, for amber waves of grain, for
purple mountains' majesty, above the fruited plain." Here,
more than anywhere else on our trip, was a landscape for
"America the Beautiful": A song that celebrates a landscape, perhaps a western landscape, possibly a Montana
landscape—a fitting song for a national anthem. A song
that portrays a harmony between a people and their land,
a Middle Landscape—a fitting image for what a nation
might attain.

52. United States border station at Piegan, Montana, northern end of U.S. 89.

The other vision typified the West as a region. It struck us as we headed south from Piegan, back down u.s. 89, the first steps on our long journey home. A few miles from the international border, we noticed an irrigation ditch. It occurred to us that we had seen ditches and canals as consistently, though in their low profiles not as conspicuously, as any landscape feature along our route—in the valley of the Santa Cruz and the city of Phoenix in Arizona, within the lowlands of the Sevier and San Pitch rivers and of the Wasatch Front in Utah, along the Salt and Snake rivers in Wyoming, and, now, on the western plains of Montana. In turn, they were a reminder of a dominant reality of the American West, one not always recognized by Americans generally or westerners specifically—the lack of abundant water. Perhaps aridity, the West as Desert, underlies many of the other images which we had seen on our trip. It has constrained the achievement of Turnerian progress and perhaps the Big Rock Candy Mountain. By discouraging growth, it has helped maintain the Frontier, the Middle Landscape, and Protected Wild Nature.

A few days after leaving the border at Piegan, we were speeding home on an eastbound interstate highway in southern Minnesota. The sky was hazy with humidity; the corn was dense and tall and endless; the trees in wood-lots, the tall grass on the road right-of-way, the cattails in the roadside marshes—all were deep green. The soil nowhere showed through the thick plant cover; bare rock broke not the horizon; and seemingly everywhere standing water glistened in innumerable puddles and ponds. We knew that we had left the Interior West, the American West, far behind.

CONCLUSIONS

Looking Back

Having completed our trip north along U.S. 89, we can now look back down the highway and consider some general observations regarding relationships between mental images and landscape scenes in the Interior West.

THE CHALLENGE OF RECONCILING THE SUBJECTIVE WITH THE OBJECTIVE

Each of the eight mental images was manifested in the landscapes along U.S. 89. The fact that no single image seemed dominant suggests the diversity of possible interpretations of the Interior West—the region as a whole defies simple, monolithic description. Yet, smaller regions crossed by U.S. 89 often did seem to have a dominant image. Never did these strongest images exist to the exclusion of others—ambiguities characterize the generalities—but areas did impress us as being distinctive. Think about the route sweeping north from Nogales: Southern and central Arizona seemed home to the Big Rock Candy Mountain—imaginary mines at Tumacacori, lost mines in the Superstition Mountains, rich mines at Jerome. Northern Arizona and extreme southern Utah particularly suggested the Desert image—limited water supply constraining human activities was a major message of the Native American ruins at Walnut Canyon, Sunset Crater, and Wupatki National Monuments for prehistoric times, and technology allegedly coping with this constraint was a theme at Glen Canyon Dam for contemporary times. Through most of Utah, the small towns, the fields of hay, and the pastures with cattle, all set within valleys bordered by forested slopes and mountain peaks, persistently suggested the Interior West as Middle Landscape. Along the entire route, large cities portrayed the progression of development according to the Turnerian formula; this image seemed particularly strong, however, for both small and large cities along Utah's Wasatch Front, where growth from a few pioneering families to small farming settlements to larger diversified towns to modern urban sprawls, all in what is commonly described as a "desert," has been proudly seen as representing the success of the Latter Day Saint spirit. The Mormon empire continues through Idaho and into Wyoming, but we found that soon after we crossed the Wyoming state line the dominant image became the Interior West as Frontier—the arch of elk antlers at Afton, the Cowboy Saloon in Jackson, and the dude ranches in Jackson Hole all being prominent symbols. In northwestern Wyoming, Grand Teton and Yellowstone National Parks represented a domination by the Protected Wild Nature image. Across Montana, a Frontier image, with livestock ranches, seemed to be mixed with a Middle Landscape image, suggested by wheat fields extending to the distant ranges of the Rockies.

The final two images, those without regional cores, occurred in a scattered pattern along the entire cross section. The Empty Quarter appeared only occasionally—especially at military bombing ranges which imply that the Interior West is most important as land to help provide security for the rest of the country—and the Playground appeared frequently, in a multitude of specific expressions.

Taken as a whole, then, the mental images portrayed in the landscape scenes of the Interior West suggest a Navajo sandpainting disturbed by a gentle wind. Within the exterior boundaries, which themselves are blurred by blown sand, the major areas formed by colors and shapes remain distinct, but their simple purity is compromised by individual grains of sand of varying color strewn across the surface.

We suspect that had we traveled other highways across the Interior West, moreover, we would have sensed the same mental images but probably in different relative importances. U.S. 95, for example, would have taken us beside at least seven bombing and gunnery ranges, ammunition depots, and other military bases of the Defense Department—a stronger suggestion of the Empty Quarter image than we encountered along U.S. 89. That same route would also have emphasized the Desert, at the expense of the Garden and Protected Wild Nature images. Regardless, however, our yearly wanderings through the Interior West for more than two decades convince us that the eight images would be part of the landscape scene no matter what route we followed. In other words, the appearance of landscapes in the Interior West seems to correspond to, and perhaps reinforce, the mental images which people have of the region.

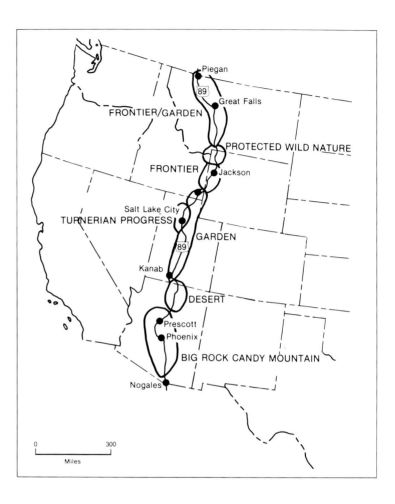

DOMINANT IMAGES. Certain images seemed dominant for areas traversed by U.S. 89.

To what degree have conscious human efforts to manifest these mental images in the landscape contributed to our sense of regionalization? Attempts to fulfill human purposes explain why landscape appearance often corresponds to a particular mental image—people have intervened to maintain or create some physical manifestation that conforms to their perceptions and attitudes. In other words, people want places in the Interior West to look as they think such places "should" look, and, when the opportunity arises to bring the mentally desired and visually perceived images to complement each other, they act accordingly. Several examples come to mind. The appearance of landscapes as wild, and wild because they are protected, is a strong image of the national parks. Therefore, policies restrict recreational facilities such as roads, stores, or lodges from national parks whether or not such

developments have any objectively definable or significant ecological impact on the environment. "Wildness"
or "naturalness" is thus a concept that may be expressed
either in landscape appearance or ecosystem functioning,
and park policy seems to indicate that the former is as
important as the latter to the American public. Also, we
observed that people often manipulated landscape scenes
to comply with the mental image of the Middle Landscape. The wish to allay the Desert prompts the building
of decorative fountains; the more intense the aridity of the
Desert the more spectacular is the display of water to
counter that image. Similarly, the plantings of native flora
in yards of subdivision homes and of palm trees along
streets in desert cities are measures taken to soften the
artifacts of humans with features of nature and thereby to
suggest a harmonious balance between the two. A similar
motivation may help to explain, in wild settings such as
national parks or exclusive subdivisions in well-to-do
neighborhoods, the design of buildings, intended to "fit
in," to be "harmonious" with the shapes, colors, and tex-
tures of the natural setting. The symbolism of the form
seems as important as the functioning of the system.

The mental image that seems to inspire the most obvious and widespread human intervention in the landscape scenes of the Interior West is that of the Frontier.
On our trips along u.s. 89, we noted the "Old West" in
names given to homes, streets, and businesses; in decorative adornments on commercial establishments; in designs of buildings; in the human history that was commemorated; in folk heroes that were created and were
eulogized; in clothing worn; in store merchandise sold; in
recreational activities promoted; in festive occasions celebrated. This tribute to a romanticized past reminds residents that their Frontier still exists, but the features particularly excite the outsiders, the newcomers, the
tourists. "Experience the land the way it used to be," the
admonition seems to be, "when the continent was fresh
and civilization was young." It is a longing for American
roots, perhaps, but its backward focus may also hint of a
dissatisfaction with the present. "Nostalgic regret," to use
Wallace Stegner's phrase, over the course of civilization
may contribute to the admiration of not only protected
wild nature but also the Frontier. Some observers have
criticized such regret as destructively anti-modern, but
our reactions are different: What is it about contemporary
life that prompts this longing for the past, even for mere
caricatures of it?

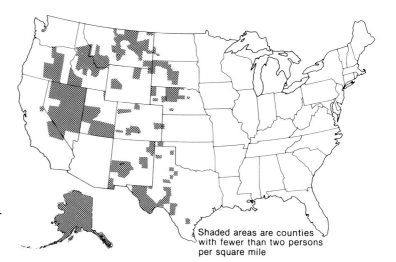

THE WEST AS FRONTIER. The sparsely settled Interior West is the region where many people seek landscapes of the American Frontier. (Map adapted from Popper 1984)

Shaded areas are counties with fewer than two persons per square mile

The degree to which the Frontier is physically manifested for the enticement of tourists is testimony to the importance of tourism as a force influencing the appearance of the land. This strength of tourism struck us as we thought about the landscape scenes and the associated imagery of Indian lands near the two extremes of U.S. 89. The Navajo lands of northern Arizona conformed well to the Frontier image: The Navajo people encourage the Frontier imagery by their colorful dress, their crafts of turquoise jewelry and blanket weaving, their dance performances, and their appearances in photographs astride horses and beside small herds of sheep. Tourists come to expect these manifestations of the Frontier on the Navajo lands. But on the Blackfeet Reservation of Montana such conscious Frontier features are unexplainably lacking; only the herds of cattle and horses and the open rangelands, neither designed to entice the tourist, suggest the Cowboy West. Nonetheless, tourism influences the Blackfeet lands, but it is an ahistorical tourism of the Playground—motels, pizza restaurants, private campgrounds. The Blackfeet seem to have chosen to promote a twentieth-century Playground, rather than an eighteenth- or nineteenth-century Frontier, to encourage their tourist economy.

The question arises, to what extent would other Americans agree with our identification of local regions, however fuzzy the margins and overlap. To suggest that landscape interpretations are *solely* a result of expectation simplifies erroneously the interplay between viewer and view. For landscapes generally, and for landscapes of the Interior West particularly, the characteristics of the visual scene suggest, prompt, encourage certain interpretations more than others. The fact that more than one interpretation of any one scene is always possible does not mean that all interpretations of all scenes are likely; ambiguity is not equivalent to chaos. There are limits to and order in landscape interpretation.

Differences among viewers help to account for differences in such interpretations. One such factor is knowledge. People may interpret landscapes of the Interior West only in terms of knowledge that they have about the region and its people-land interactions; in other words, people can see only those meanings, those mental images, for which they have knowledge. Education about some of the images may come from informal sources, such as newspapers or television; this sort of education seems sufficient to learn about such images as the Frontier or the Playground. Other images may require more formal education or more sophisticated information; examples might include the environmental degradation associated with the Desert image or the outside economic controls associated with the Empty Quarter image. In particular, the realization that the images may be as much myth as reality seems to require more insightful knowledge; understanding helps landscape viewers to appreciate aridity as a limit to the manifestation of the Garden and to see the constraints of resource availability on the development of the Big Rock Candy Mountain.

A second difference among individuals that helps to account for variations in landscape interpretation is the status of the viewer as either resident "insider" or visiting "outsider." This source of novelty in perspective may help to explain why incompatible mental images are seen in a single landscape by different people. Examples are common. The meadows within Yellowstone National Park may be seen as Protected Wild Nature by vacationing visitors but as Empty Quarter exploitation by the ranchers whose cattle graze along the barbed-wire boundary. An irrigated, Arizona cotton farm may be viewed as a veritable Eden by its proud owner, but as a mere superficial oasis of the Desert by some outsiders. A town like Jackson, Wyoming, may seem to be part of the Frontier by outsiders anxious to be part of the Cowboy myth, but to be a frivolous Playground for the wealthy by insiders, knowingly catering to the tourists' illusions. Citizens of Phoenix, Arizona, may envision themselves as living in a kind of harmonious Middle Landscape, but outsiders might see the landscape as an expression of the domination of culture over nature, as a completion of the Turnerian Progression.

Still another factor that helps to account for differences in landscape interpretation is variable human purpose, variation in the purposes that individuals think landscape should serve. Merchants in a small town of a Utah mountain valley, for example, might feel that their purposes for economic security are best served by growth in business, and thus they would look favorably upon landscape imagery suggesting the Big Rock Candy Mountain or the Turnerian Progression and unfavorably upon manifestations of the wealth-draining influences of the Empty Quarter. Farmers elsewhere in the same valley, on the other hand, might value more strongly the image of the Garden and thus lament the growing commercial strip at the edge of town. A local environmentalist, finally, might see the Desert image in the gully development downstream from the farmer's fields.

Complicating these influences on landscape interpretation are the multiple purposes, even conflicting purposes, that are part of all people. For example, at the same time that the merchants desire the economic successes associated with Turnerian growth, they may yearn for the small-town intimacy of the Middle Landscape or hope for the gentle consumptive uses of nature that permit a rich and productive biota for hunting or fishing or bird watching. Humans must always cope with their inconsistencies and contradictions.

THE FUTURE

Such variable purposes complicate everyone's life and render human behavior inconsistent, but individual and societal purposes must be articulated and evaluated before landscape characteristics that are considered most desirable and most important can be identified and then preserved or created. One logical extension of this preservation or creation of desired images into the future is to establish a series of "theme parks," each intended to preserve a particular image of the West. Such measures may not be as outrageous as they first appear. National parks already may be seen as an effort to regionalize a Protected Wild Nature, and concentrations of resorts and other tourist attractions—the Black Hills come to mind—represent a regionalization of the Playground. Other examples are less explicit but no less real: Financial subsidies of range forage on public lands and federal programs for range improvements are efforts to make possible what is often an uneconomic range livestock industry in the "Frontier" of Wyoming and Nevada. Similarly, federal farm policies are often motivated by a desire to maintain the harmony of the family farm in the threatening face of corporate farms—will suggestions be made to allow economic forces to continue their march toward consolidation and corporate management generally, but to "save" the Middle Landscape of the family farm in particular regions where it remains, perhaps in small-town, Mormon Utah?

The human effort to create or maintain manifestations of mental images in landscapes often is complicated by multiple human purposes—people attempt to merge more than one mental image in a given landscape scene, and this effort is hampered or frustrated by the incompatibility of certain combinations of the images. For example, the Middle Landscape image is inconsistent with the completion of the Turnerian Progression; yet, people living in small towns often welcome economic growth that will enhance their standards of living and encourage their children to remain close to home, even though such change will necessarily threaten what they perceive to be the benefits of their Middle Landscape existence. These threats were being experienced in many towns along our route of travel—Sedona, Delta, and Jackson readily come to mind—where a harmonious balance between nature and culture in a Middle Landscape seems imperiled.

Other combinations of mental images raise similar questions: Can a people maintain a Frontier while pursuing the benefits of a Big Rock Candy Mountain? Can a Frontier remain viable while it caters to those who want a Playground? Can a landscape dedicated to Protecting Wild Nature also serve as a Playground?

This third question particularly impressed us in the national parks of Wyoming. The National Park Service attempts to preserve wild landscapes in units of the National Park System while it also offers, even encourages, those same units as Playgrounds. It is no wonder that visitors are confused. They come from the Playground atmosphere of Jackson Hole's dude ranches, where they swim, ride horses, play tennis or golf, enjoy trail rides and western cookouts, and enter Yellowstone, where they encounter a generally more wild environment. When they find bison on the roadside, it is not surprising that they react as if the animals are docile denizens of a petting-zoo, rather than unpredictable beasts of wild nature. The in-

COMPATIBILITY OF IMAGES. Combinations of images may not be compatible in the same landscape. (Don Wright editorial cartoon reprinted by permission: Tribune Media Services)

creased number of bison gorings that we heard about when we passed through Yellowstone might reflect a mental image of national parks as Playgrounds, an image that the Park Service itself has fostered.

This suggestion of the importance of the role of the Playground image in the national parks' overall function raises a new question about the responses of the National Park Service to its traditional dilemma of how to balance its dual goals of providing for recreation and providing a protected nature to cultivate the public's "contemplative faculty" (Sax 1980). The Park Service has generally prohibited many recreational activities, such as horse racing and water skiing, as detracting from the contemplation of nature in its wild state. Recently, it has attempted further to regulate outdoor recreation activities—the size of groups camping in back country areas has been limited; the use of artificial stocking of fish to improve angling success has been eliminated; activities such as Yellowstone's begging bears or Yosemite's firefall have been curtailed or discontinued. A common argument for taking these measures is that the activities are not consistent with the Protected Wild Nature image and that their elimination will improve the visitors' appreciation of nature. Yet, the Park Service promotes other recreational activities, for example, bicycle riding, rock climbing, and white-water rafting. Since the Park Service's reasons for promoting these are not articulated, a logical assumption could be that the Park Service believes that they foster a closer human relationship with wildness. But when one considers that these activities often appeal to visitors interested in endurance-testing or thrill-seeking more than in the understanding or appreciation of wild nature, a question arises as to the results of, if not the real motivations for, the agency's actions. Has the Park Service truly identified a group of Playground activities through which the practitioners will appreciate wild nature better than their predecessors who caught the planted trout or fed the roadside bears? Or have they promoted them as "good" merely because of their low impacts on Wild Nature? A public that wants a part in the decision-making process concerning its public lands needs to be aware of the questions before it can determine the answers.

Whether the reason behind the manifestation of any particular mental image in the landscape scene is one of human intervention or of natural forces, or both, such manifestation is augmented by the human capacity for imagination, which encourages the perception of meanings in the visual scene. A perception might not, however, correspond to reality. The eight mental images are not equally true when subjected to objective evaluations. The Interior West is not a blank and homogeneous plain, capable of manifesting equally each of the mental images.

Consider, for example, the validity of the expression of the Interior West as the Big Rock Candy Mountain. To what degree is the Interior West a treasure box of natural resources waiting to be opened and economic opportunities waiting to be grabbed? For many resources, particularly some associated strongly with the Interior West, the answer is that the region is not a cornucopia. For example, the National Petroleum Council (1972) has estimated that only 12 percent of the country's ultimate production of petroleum would come from what they called the "Rocky Mountain Region," an area which extends from Minnesota southwest to Arizona. Moreover, the Council suggested that only 17 percent of the petroleum then yet to be discovered would come from that region, an amount comparable to that which was yet to be discovered in the leading oil-producing state of Texas. The overthrust belt, then, will not solve the problem of declining domestic production of petroleum, no matter how strong the visions and the contentions of the Big Rock Candy Mountain dreamers may be. Developers can no more succeed in pumping their pipelines full of petroleum by wishful thinking than the owners of the Big Rock Candy Mountain Resort in Utah could succeed in their lemonade

springs by laying plastic pipe. The appearance of the landscape along U.S. 89 confirmed the reality: The petroleum
reserves of the famed overthrust belt of the northern
Rocky Mountains were hardly visible.

Similarly, we observed logging activity in the landscapes of the Interior West, but, again appropriately, it was
not prominent: Only 7 percent of the nation's most productive commercial timberland is in the Rocky Mountains (U.S. Forest Service 1976). The timber industry will
continue to be concentrated in those regional environments better suited to the growing of trees, the Southeast
and the Pacific Northwest, which account for two-thirds
of the best timberland in the country.

A common perception of the Interior West as a rich
Frontier, where countless herds of cattle are rounded up
to transport to eastern markets, is also contrary to the
facts, for livestock of the western range represents but a
minor part of the system of livestock production in the
United States. The forage produced in the Interior West is
only about 14 percent of the total forage consumed by
livestock in the United States, and much of this total
probably comes from improved pastures rather than open
rangelands (Vale 1979). In contrast to the two previous
cases, however, here the western landscape with its vast
stretches of both rangeland and unimproved pasture
would seem to belie the statistics, unless an astute observer would notice, as our text confirms, that although
livestock were frequent they were not abundant.

The Interior West, however, does spill some riches.
Ironically, they probably are least recognizable as such by
the casual traveler. The volumes of coal on the northern
plains and in the northern Rocky Mountains are immense; three-fourths of the nation's ultimate production
of coal might come from these regions. Yet the primary
manifestations of this wealth along U.S. 89 were short
strings of railroad coal cars and occasional coal-laden
trucks in Utah. Another profitable enterprise, the promoting of western amenities, particularly the positive mental images as manifested in landscapes, is luring increasing numbers of retirees and vacationers to all parts of the
Interior West. A thoughtful line from the movie based on
Farley Mowatt's *Never Cry Wolf* (1973) was the observation by a would-be entrepreneur that the "real wealth" of
the wild Arctic was the potential tourist, "home in front
of the television set," rather than the potential mineral
riches beneath the frozen soil of the Big Rock Candy
Mountain of the continental Frontier. In addition, the In-

terior West, for reasons both environmental and political, enjoys the economic benefits of disproportionately large defense spending, whether for the development or manufacturing of weapons or for the testing, storage, and deployment of them.

In sum, the Interior West as Big Rock Candy Mountain is only partially valid, and perhaps more for services than for commodity resources. Regardless of the ambiguities, belief in the image draws aliens over the border fence from Mexico in ever-increasing numbers and encourages out-of-work refugees from the Northeast to hazard hopeful, but often fruitless, trips to the Southwest. For them, as for the country's population collectively—a population that looks to its future supply of resources—an objective evaluation is useful. Belief in a Big Rock Candy Mountain image that is not true is belief that courts disaster.

A similar analysis might illuminate the contrary perspectives of the Interior West as agricultural Garden and as unreclaimable Desert. A favorite theme for historians of American attitudes and perceptions, this dichotomy of contradictory interpretations of the West, usually made murky by human imagination, can be clarified by simple, objective facts: Precipitation is less abundant, less evenly distributed, and less reliable in the Interior West than in the humid East; the Interior West cannot escape its dryness, and the heavily tapped bounty of the Colorado River is hardly sufficient to blanket the West with the verdure of the Midwest Garden.

Disparity between mental image and physical reality, however, need not always have negative consequences; myths may have positive effects, as well. Consider Grand Teton National Park and the blemishes that it presents as a manifestation of the image of Protected Wild Nature. The dam, the livestock grazing, the airport, and the elk hunting represent deviations from the ideal of a wild landscape preserve. Cynics can point to these examples as evidence of the fundamental falsehood of the image; that is, these people might say, it is a myth to claim that Americans have protected wild nature as a resource. Yet, for those who value parks and wild nature, it is important not to dismiss the inconsistencies as proof of the greed or hypocrisy of people generally or of American society specifically. Belief in the tradition of saving wild nature, even if flawed, facilitates the goals of wild nature protection. By choosing to claim this somewhat adulterated remnant of nature's beauty and elevate it to the status of a national park icon, we not only save it from further deformity but also ensure the opportunity for more citizens to develop an appreciation for the wild nature in it. Compromising the myth, in this case, ensures its persistence in reality as at least partial truth.

The protection of wild nature represents an image of landscape in which a certain state or condition, albeit a dynamic one, is preserved. Several other images similarly involve persistence of a given circumstance; the Frontier, the Garden, and the Playground are examples of such images that might be termed "structural." Still other images, however, embody change—the Turnerian Progression, Empty Quarter, and Big Rock Candy Mountain envision development of resources and growth of communities; these might be described as "process" images. The pace of change in modern American society seems to favor the process images, and those reacting against development, against modernization, against growth often advocate a persistence of the structural images. There may be need to create new images, or novel combinations of factors in existing images, in which the favorable characteristics of the structural images can be maintained or enhanced in a world of changing landscapes.

Are the forces of change which are intrinsic to the process images so dominant and so common that the landscapes of the Interior West are becoming increasingly similar? It is a popular conception that throughout the Interior West, as elsewhere, the modernization and spread of corporate America has reduced the local variability in such landscape features as economic activities, housing characteristics, and retail stores. True, there are places where motels and RV parks have supplanted the farms and ranches from Arizona to Montana; where resorts and condominiums of rock and concrete and glass have replaced the adobe of the Southwest, the brick of Mormon Utah, and the wooden frames of Montana; where the McDonald's and Denny's have crowded out the mom and pop cafes in small towns and large cities alike. Over the short term, these changes may actually increase the diversity of landscape character by mixing the traditional and modern, the old and the new, the local and the national. Over the long term, however, a continuation of modern trends portends a loss of much of the variability in the human institutions that give character to western landscapes.

Spatial scale confuses the question of whether or not landscape character in the Interior West is becoming increasingly homogenized. For example, a commercial strip in Phoenix may be indistinguishable from one in Salt

Lake City if the view is of the immediate street and its stores, or the view of an alley may evoke the same response whether in Flagstaff or Great Falls. But a slightly larger frame of reference might bring into view a corner of the bare red rock of Papago Park or the snow-covered summits of the Wasatch Range; it might include a backdrop of the San Francisco Peaks or the open range of the Great Plains. Any of these larger perspectives would help identify the place as particular and as western. The maintenance of distinctiveness in landscape seems a desirable goal, but the continuation of such unique character is probably increasingly difficult on an immediate and local scale. Such distinctiveness requires attention to landscape form that encourages perception of regional images.

In both the Interior West specifically and the West generally, wild nature seems a critically distinctive element for regional landscapes and regional mental images of the region. In the Protected Wild Nature image, it is a wild nature preserved from development. In many manifestations of the Big Rock Candy Mountain and the Empty Quarter images, it is a beckoning, bountiful, unprotected wild nature of rich and untapped, but tappable, wealth. In the Middle Landscape and Frontier images, it is the autonomous and unfettered wild nature that is the contrasting backdrop for the discipline of human economies. In the Playground image, it is frequently an untamed setting for outdoor recreation. In the Desert image, it is the wild nature of areas undeveloped and not visited because undevelopable and not admired by humans. An expansive and conspicuous wild nature, more than any other landscape element, may be the necessary ingredient for the Interior West to remain the West.

For most of the mental images and landscape scenes, then, wild nature is vital. To the degree that this is true, the character of the Interior West is threatened by growth, by realization of the "process" images. Economic growth usually is perceived as a threat to Protected Wild Nature because commercial development is typically inconsistent with wild landscapes. But more generally, growth seems to consume the wild nature present in the Frontier, the Middle Landscape, and the Desert. In these cases, it is a consumption of wild nature by the successes of the Big Rock Candy Mountain, the Empty Quarter, and, sometimes, the Playground which threatens a perpetuation of wildness in the landscape; these changes are often directional, in Turnerian terms, although the ghost towns of past mining booms should suggest that such changes may

WILD NATURE. Wild nature is an essential element in most images of the Interior West, in most regional landscapes of the American West. In this figure, the importance of wild nature in each mental image, or in landscape manifestations of each image, is estimated: In Protected Wild Nature, the image and landscape are mostly free of human activities and artifacts; the Frontier has a dominant wild nature as the backdrop for the little developed world of humans, and the Desert portrays a dominant wild nature because aridity precludes intensive human use; the Middle Landscape, the Garden, presents an equal balance between the natural and human worlds; a subdominant role for wild nature characterizes the Playground, in which wild settings are only part of the recreational scene, the Big Rock Candy Mountain, in which undeveloped resources contribute to a vision of future riches, and the Empty Quarter, in which wildness in the land is sometimes seen as exploited by outside interests; for the Turnerian Progression, the wild landscape is the base, often a memory, from which the contemporary, human-dominated world has been formed.

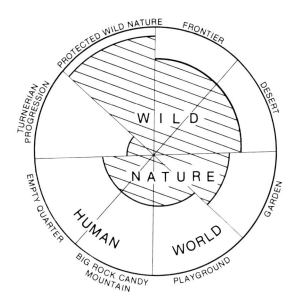

also be cyclical. Most menacing of all to wild nature is the completion of the Turner Progression and the development of urban centers in which wild nature is at best a remnant element in a mostly humanized environment. Perhaps the greatest threat to the character of the Interior West, then, comes not from resource extraction, whether it is dam building, cattle grazing, or coal mining, because these activities often may be pursued in wild settings, but rather from expansion of trailer parks, suburban developments, shopping malls, commercial strips, second homes, and urban renewals. These changes create landscapes which are the least distinctly "western," and thus threaten the most common impressions of, and perhaps the most desired futures for, the region. In other words, increased numbers of people, more than resource development, *per se*, may be the greatest threat to perpetuation of the character of the Interior West.

The protection of wild nature in parks and wilderness areas is the best guarantee for maintaining wildness in the landscapes of the Interior West, but such action cannot perpetuate the wild nature that is essential to other mental images of the region. In fact, the creation of nature reserves is a mixed blessing: While it ensures the protection of wild landscapes from development, it also eliminates the unbounded character that is part of true wildness. Perhaps unprotected wild nature is the most threatened landscape element because fewer and fewer parts of the Interior West are escaping the scrutiny of the creators of wild nature reserves or the developers of economic wealth. Every part of the region, it seems, is being quarreled over; every proposal, whether for a park or a wilderness area, for a grazing allotment or a new mine, generates controversy. This fact reflects the "fullness" of the American land, to use Daniel Luten's (1969) phrase, in which multiple, overlapping claims on the landscape extend onto every mountain valley and into every desert ravine. As admirers of wild nature, and as students of western landscapes, we can only approve proposals for increased protection of wild landscapes, but we also feel some sadness when the empty spaces on the maps of the Interior West are filled with new roads, new settlements, new mines, and, even, new parks.

A "filling" of the West to match the dense settlement in the East may never occur because of the distinctiveness of nature in the West, especially the Interior West: The rugged mountains and, especially, the arid climates may continue to discourage more intensive human use. Explicit and graceful acceptance of these natural constraints to human activity will contribute to, and are necessary to, wise relationships between people and land in the West.

The natural conditions of rugged terrain and dry climate help to maintain the wildness that may be a critical element in the distinctiveness of western landscapes. In the West, more than in more humid parts of the country, the character of nature plays an essential role in identifying regional landscapes; here, the primacy of individual perception as a sole determinant of landscape interpretation is untenable. Whether in the tangible human use of landscape or in the intangible human interpretation of landscape, then, the wildness in landscape, wildness born of mountains and aridity, is distinctively western.

To assume that natural conditions will maintain regional landscapes of the Interior West is naive—human agency and human institutions will continue to help form the western landscapes into the future. Americans ought to be aware of the consequences of the choices that they are making about the future of this region, choices of action or of neglect, choices influenced or dictated by mental images, lest they discover that they have created landscape scenes which they find neither physically sustainable nor socially, culturally, or emotionally desirable.

Our personal vision of those landscapes emphasizes diversity of images and meanings: We hope for more parks and wilderness but also for continued irrigated alfalfa fields and grazing Hereford cattle; sustained clearcut logging and persistent open-pit copper mining; successful art galleries, restaurants, and RV campgrounds for the tourists, and desolate, empty, and unused desert for those who love to see, or think about, true wildness. We want bustling metropolises to continue to be bustling, and small, quiet towns to continue to be small and quiet. We envision a West whose landscapes reflect persistence and continuity more than growth and change.

In the first quarter of this century, F. Scott Fitzgerald (1925) chronicled for the East the inexorable path of a society from the "fresh, green" promise of mystery and beauty to ashen wasteland when its "romantic readiness," however strong, is founded on illusion. Here in the West, in the last quarter of that same century, let us infuse America's "extraordinary gift for hope" with an understanding and acceptance of reality, so that we may "beat on," boats *with* the current, into a visionary future "commensurate to [our] capacity for wonder."

The future landscapes of the Interior West cannot be anything and everything, but they can be different things. Better land-use planning, better ecological understanding, and better economic and social institutions will each help mold the best for the West, but what is really needed is a vision of the future, a vision of what future western landscapes can and should be.

References

Numerous sources, both scholarly and popular, formal and informal, were consulted in writing the book. Only those sources quoted or specifically mentioned in the text are listed here.

ABBEY, EDWARD
  1968   *Desert Solitaire.* New York: McGraw-Hill.
  1975   *The Monkey Wrench Gang.* Philadelphia: J. B. Lippincott.
  1982   "The Phoenix Type" (letter). *Arizona Daily Star* (Tucson), December 21.
  1985   "Navajos" (letter). *American West* 22(1):20.
ALEXANDER, THOMAS
  1979   "Ogden: A Federal Colony in Utah." *Utah Historical Quarterly* 47: 290–309.
ALLARD, WILLIAM
  1982   *Vanishing Breed: Photographs of the Cowboy and the West.* Boston: Little, Brown, and Company.
ARIAV, ALAN
  1984   "Penniless mom had one desire: A ticket home" and "Couple came here with hope but left broke." *Arizona Republic* (Phoenix), January 2.
BAILEY, ROBERT G.
  1978   Description of Ecoregions of the United States. Ogden, Utah: U. S. Department of Agriculture, Forest Service.
BASSETT, CAROL ANN
  1985   "After the Big Fire in Next-Year Country." *American West* 22(1):26–33.
BERGON, FRANK, AND ZEESE PAPANIKOLAS
  1978   *Looking Far West: The Search for the American West in History, Myth, and Literature.* New York: Mentor.
BIGGAR, JEANNE
  1979   "The Sunning of America: Migration to the Sunbelt." *Population Bulletin* 34. Washington, D.C.: Population Reference Bureau.
BINGHAM, WAYNE, AND JOSEPH LINTON
  1983   "Why not make a stream downtown?" *Deseret News* (Salt Lake City), June 26.
BOYER, RICHARD, AND DAVID SAVAGEAN
  1985   *Places Rated Almanac.* Chicago: Rand McNally.

BREWER, JAMES
   1983   *Jerome: A Story of Mines, Men, and Money.* Globe,
          Arizona: Southwest Parks and Monument Associa-
          tion.
BUREAU OF LAND MANAGEMENT
   1985   *South Dakota Resource Area, Resource Manage-
          ment Plan, Environmental Impact Statement,
          Draft.* Billings, Montana: Bureau of Land Manage-
          ment.
   1987   *Paria Canyon-Vermilion Cliffs Wilderness Manage-
          ment Plan, Final.* St. George, Utah: Bureau of Land
          Management.
BUREAU OF RECLAMATION
   1964   "From Out of the West." *Reclamation Era* 50(1):5–
          9.
BURT, NATHANIEL
   1983   *Jackson Hole Journal.* Norman: University of Okla-
          homa Press.
BURT, WILLIAM
   1976   *A Field Guide to the Mammals.* Boston: Houghton-
          Mifflin.
CAMPBELL, ROBERT
   1983   "To a visiting Easterner, Phoenix is a formless void
          best avoided." *Tucson Citizen,* December 17.
CANADIAN WILDLIFE SERVICE/U.S. FISH AND WILDLIFE SERVICE
   1986   *North American Waterfowl Management Plan.* Ot-
          tawa: Canadian Wildlife Service.
CARLTON, MICHAEL
   1983   ". . . A tale of two parks." *Denver Post,* July 31.
CATHER, WILLA
   1913   *O Pioneers!* Boston: Houghton-Mifflin.
   1918   *My Antonia.* London: W. Heinemann.
   1927   *Death Comes For the Archbishop.* New York: Mod-
          ern Library.
CHAPMAN, JOSEPH, AND GEORGE FELDHAMER
   1982   *Wild Mammals of North America.* Baltimore: Johns
          Hopkins University Press.
CHENEY, ROBERTA CARKEEK
   1971   *Names on the Face of Montana.* Missoula: Univer-
          sity of Montana.
   1983   *Names on the Face of Montana.* Missoula: Moun-
          tain Press Publishing Company.
COMEAUX, MALCOLM
   1981   *Arizona.* Boulder, Colorado: Westview Press.
CONLEY, CORT
   1982   *Idaho for the Curious.* Cambridge, Idaho: Backeddy
          Books.
DAWSON, PATRICK
   1987   "'Big Open' Proposal Arouses Strong Emotion
          and Hostility in Montana." *High Country News*
          19(21):14–15.

DEVOTO, BERNARD
  1934   "The West: A Plundered Province." *Harpers* 169 (August):355–364.
DYSON, JAMES
  1960   *The Geologic Story of Glacier National Park.* West Glacier, Montana: Glacier Natural History Association.
EHRLICH, GRETEL
  1985   *The Solace of Open Spaces.* New York: Viking.
FEDERAL WRITERS' PROJECT
  1938   *The Idaho Encyclopedia.* Caldwell, Idaho: Caxton Printers.
FITZGERALD, F. SCOTT
  1925   *The Great Gatsby.* New York: Grosset and Dunlap.
GARREAU, JOEL
  1981   *The Nine Nations of North America.* Boston: Houghton-Mifflin.
GOETZMANN, WILLIAM
  1981   "The Awesome Space in Time," pp. 55–60 in E. Richard Hart, ed., *That Awesome Space.* Salt Lake City: Westwater Press.
GRANGER, BYRD HOWELL
  1983   *Arizona's Names: X Marks the Place.* Tucson: Falconer Publishing.
GRAY, RALPH, AND JAMES BLAIR
  1964   "From Sun-Clad Sea to Shining Mountains." *National Geographic* 125(4):542–89.
GREAT FALLS TRIBUNE
  1983   "State Livestock Department Battling New Brand of Rustlers," August 7.
GRESSLEY, GENE M.
  1977   "Colonialism and the American West," pp. 31–47 in Gene Gressley, *The Twentieth-Century American West.* Columbia: University of Missouri Press.
GREY, ZANE
  1912   *Riders of the Purple Sage.* New York: Grosset and Dunlap.
GUNTHER, JOHN
  1947   *Inside U.S.A.* New York: Harper and Brothers.
GUTHRIE, A. B.
  1947   *The Big Sky.* New York: William Sloane.
  1949   *The Way West.* New York: William Sloane.
  1970   *Arfive.* New York: Houghton-Mifflin.
HALL, ANDY
  1983   "Out in the Cold. The Homeless: A Year Later, Phoenix, U.S. No Better Off." *Arizona Republic* (Phoenix), December 18.
HAMILTON, JOHN, AND JOHN BATCHELOR
  1987   *Thunder in the Dust: Classic Images of Western Movies.* New York: Stewart, Tabori, and Chang.

HELLER, NANCY, AND JULIA WILLIAMS
    1982   *Painters of the American Scene.* New York: Gala-
            had Books.

HOLLON, W. EUGENE
    1966   *The Great American Desert.* New York: Oxford
            University Press.

HUMPHREY, R. R.
    1987   *90 Years and 535 Miles: Vegetation Changes Along
            the Mexican Border.* Albuquerque: University of
            New Mexico Press.

HUMPHREY, R. R., AND L. A. MEHRHOFF
    1958   "Vegetation Changes on a Southern Arizona Grass-
            land Range." *Ecology* 39:720–26.

HUNT, CHARLES
    1976   *Natural Regions of the United States and Canada.*
            San Francisco: W. H. Freeman.

ISE, JOHN
    1961   *Our National Park Policy.* Baltimore: Johns Hop-
            kins University Press.

JACKSON, RICHARD, AND ROBERT LAYTON
    1976   "The Mormon Village: Analysis of a Settlement
            Type." *Professional Geographer* 28:136–41.

KITTREDGE, WILLIAM
    1987   *Owning It All.* St. Paul: Graywolf Press.

KLUCKHOHN, CLYDE, AND DOROTHEA LEIGHTON
    1946   *The Navajo.* Republished 1962, New York: Ameri-
            can Museum of Natural History.

LAJEUNESSE, WILLIAM
    1984   "Fiesta Parade bowls 'em over." *Phoenix Sun,* Janu-
            ary 1.

LAMM, RICHARD, AND MICHAEL MCCARTHY
    1982   *The Angry West: A Vulnerable Land and Its Future.*
            Boston: Houghton-Mifflin.

LARSON, T. A.
    1977   *Wyoming: A Bicentennial History.* New York:
            W. W. Norton.

LOBECK, A. K.
    1950   *Physiographic Diagram of North America.* Maple-
            wood, New Jersey: Geographical Press (Hammond).

LOMAX, ALAN
    1960   *The Folk Songs of North America.* Garden City,
            New York: Doubleday.

LOWENTHAL, DAVID
    1968   "The American Scene." *Geographical Review*
            58:61–88.

LUTEN, DANIEL
    1966   "Engines in the Wilderness." *Landscape* 15 (3): 25–
            27.
    1969   "Empty Land, Full Land, Poor Folk, Rich Folk."
            *Yearbook of the Association of Pacific Coast Geog-
            raphers* 31:79–89.

MCGRATH, ROGER
  1984   *Gunfighters, Highwaymen, and Vigilantes.* Berkeley: University of California Press.

MARSTON, ED
  1988   "Ultimately, only the West can save the West." *High Country News* 20(2):15.

MARTIN, RUSSELL
  1983   *Cowboy, The Enduring Myth of the Wild West.* New York: Stewart, Tabori, and Chang.

MEINIG, D. W.
  1965   "The Mormon Culture Region: Strategies and Patterns in the Geography of the American West, 1847–1964." *Annals of the Association of American Geographers* 55:191–220.
  1979   "The Beholding Eye," pp. 33–48 in D. W. Meinig, ed., *The Interpretation of Ordinary Landscapes.* New York: Oxford University Press.

MIX, PAUL
  1972   *The Life and Legend of Tom Mix.* South Brunswick: A. S. Barnes.

MORGAN, DALE
  1966   "The Fur Trade and Its Historians." *Minnesota History* 40:151–56.

MORGAN, NEIL
  1961   *Westward Tilt: The American West Today.* New York: Random House.

MOWAT, FARLEY
  1973   *Never Cry Wolf.* New York: Bantam Books.

MUIR, JOHN
  1913   *The Mountains of California.* New York: Century.

NATIONAL ATLAS OF THE UNITED STATES OF AMERICA
  1970   Washington, D.C.: Geological Survey.

NATIONAL PETROLEUM COUNCIL
  1972   *U.S. Energy Outlook.* Washington, D.C.: National Petroleum Council.

NATIONS, DALE, AND EDMUND STUMP
  1983   *Geology of Arizona.* Dubuque, Iowa: Kendall Hunt.

NUKEWATCH
  n.d.   "Missile Silos of Montana" (postcard). Madison, Wisconsin: Nukewatch.

O'GARA, GEOFFREY
  1988   "The West is Burning (But it's probably good news)." *High Country News* 20(15):8–9.

OMANG, JOANNE
  1981   "Oil, Coal, MX—Too Much for Utah?" *San Francisco Chronicle,* January 11.

PEIRCE, NEIL
  1973   "Montana: High, Wide, Handsome–and Remote," pp. 474–515 in Michael Malone and Richard Roeder, eds., *Montana's Past: Selected Essays.* Missoula: University of Montana.

PETERSON, CHARLES

1977   *Utah: A Bicentennial History.* New York: W. W. Norton.

1979a   "Urban Utah: Toward a Fuller Understanding." *Utah Historical Quarterly* 47:227–35.

1979b   "Utah's Regions, A View From the Hinterland." *Utah Historical Quarterly.* 47:103–9.

1979c   "The Valley of the Bear River and the Movement of Culture Between Utah and Idaho." *Utah Historical Quarterly* 47:194–214.

POPPER, FRANK

1984   "Survival of the American Frontier." *Resources* (Resources for the Future), no. 77, (Summer):1–4.

POWELL, JOHN WESLEY

1878   *Report on the Lands of the Arid Region of the United States.* Reprinted in 1962 with editorial comments by Wallace Stegner. Cambridge: Belknap Press of Harvard University Press.

POWELL, LAWRENCE CLARK

1976   *Arizona: A Bicentennial History.* New York: W. W. Norton.

PUBLIC LAND LAW REVIEW COMMISSION

1970   *One Third of the Nation's Land.* Washington, D.C.: Government Printing Office.

PYNE, STEPHEN

1981   "Western Time and Western History," pp. 68–77 in E. Richard Hart, ed., *That Awesome Space.* Salt Lake City: Westwater Press.

RED ROCK NEWS (SEDONA, ARIZONA)

1983   "Three points of view, not two, reader says," January 5; "Proposed Indian Gardens Project Discussed," December 28.

REDFORD, ROBERT

1976   *The Outlaw Trail.* New York: Grosset and Dunlap.

RHODES-JONES, CAROLYN

1979   "Transcontinental Travelers' Excursions to Salt Lake City and Ogden: A Photographic Essay." *Utah Historical Quarterly* 47: 273–89.

RIGHTER, ROBERT

1982   *Crucible for Conservation: The Creation of Grand Teton National Park.* Denver: Colorado Associated University Press.

ROBBINS, JIM

1987   "Beauty, Isolation, and Cheapland Bring a Sect to Montana." *High Country News* 19(17):1, 8–14.

ROLVAAG, O. E.

1927   *Giants in the Earth.* New York: Harper.

ROMME, W. H., AND D. H. KNIGHT

1982   "Landscape Diversity: The Concept Applied to Yellowstone National Park." *BioScience* 32: 664–70.

ROYLANCE, WARD

    1982   *Utah, A Guide to the State.* Salt Lake City: A Guide to the State Foundation.

RUNTE, ALFRED

    1979   *National Parks: The American Experience.* Lincoln: University of Nebraska Press.

SADLER, RICHARD

    1979   "The Impact of Mining on Salt Lake City." *Utah Historical Quarterly* 47:236–53.

SAMPSON, ARTHUR, AND BERYL JESPERSEN

    1963   "California Range Brushlands and Browse Plants." *Manual 33.* Berkeley: California Agricultural Experiment Station.

SATTERFIELD, ARCHIE, AND DAVID MUENCH

    1978   *Lewis and Clark Country.* Portland, Oregon: Beautiful America Publishing.

SAVAGE, WILLIAM, ED.

    1975   *Cowboy Life: Reconstructing an American Myth.* Norman: University of Oklahoma Press.

SAX, JOSEPH

    1980   *Mountains Without Handrails.* Ann Arbor: University of Michigan.

SCHMIDT, JOHN, AND DOUGLAS GILBERT

    1978   *Big Game of North America.* Harrisburg, Pennsylvania: Stackpole.

SCHULTHEIS, ROBERT

    1983   *The Hidden West: Journeys in the American Outback.* San Francisco: North Point Press.

SHERIDAN, DAVID

    1981   *Desertification of the United States.* Washington, D. C.: Government Printing Office.

SMITH, HENRY NASH

    1950   *Virgin Land: The American West as Symbol and Myth.* Cambridge: Harvard University Press.

SNOW, DON

    1988   "Equity." *Northern Lights* 4(3):10–18.

SONNICHSEN, C. L.

    1982   *Tucson: The Life and Times of an American City.* Norman: University of Oklahoma Press.

SPENCE, CLARK

    1978   *Montana: A Bicentennial History.* New York: W. W. Norton.

STEGNER, PAGE

    1981   "The New Riders of the Purple Sage," pp. 128, 161–65 in Stegner, Wallace, and Page Stegner, *American Places.* New York: Elsevier-Dutton.

STEGNER, WALLACE

    1943   *Big Rock Candy Mountain.* New York: Duell, Sloan, and Pearce.

    1962a   *Report on the Lands of the Arid Region of the United States, by John Wesley Powell.* Cambridge, Massachusetts: Harvard University Press.

1962b   *Wolf Willow: A History, A Story, and a Memory of the Last Plains Frontier.* New York: Viking.

1971   *Angle of Repose.* Garden City, New York: Doubleday.

STEINER, STAN

1984   "Riders of the Range." *Natural History* 93(2):84–91.

STEWART, GEORGE R.

1953   *U.S. 40.* New York: Houghton-Mifflin.

1962   *The California Trail.* New York: McGraw-Hill.

TUAN, YI-FU

1959   "Pediments in Southeastern Arizona." *University of California Publications in Geography,* vol. 13. Berkeley: University of California Press.

1971   *Man and Nature.* Washington, D.C.: Association of American Geographers.

TURNER, FREDERICK JACKSON

1894   "The Significance of the Frontier in American History. *Annual Report for the Year 1893.* Washington, D.C.: American Historical Association.

UNITED STATES FOREST SERVICE

1976   *The Nation's Renewable Resources: An Assessment, 1975.* Washington, D.C.: Government Printing Office.

UNITED STATES WATER RESOURCES COUNCIL

1978   *The Nation's Water Resources, 1975–2000.* Washington, D.C.: Government Printing Office.

URBANEK, MAE

1974   *Wyoming Place Names.* Boulder, Colorado: Johnson Publishing Company.

UTAH WRITERS' PROJECT

1940   *Origins of Utah Place Names.* Salt Lake City: Utah State Department of Public Instruction.

VALE, THOMAS

1979   "Use of Public Rangelands in the American West." *Environmental Conservation* 6: 53–62.

VALE, THOMAS, ED.

1986   *Progress Against Growth: Daniel B. Luten on the American Landscape.* New York: Guilford Press.

VALE, THOMAS, AND GERALDINE VALE

1983   *U.S. 40 Today: Thirty Years of Landscape Change in America.* Madison: University of Wisconsin Press.

VANCE, JAMES

1972   "California and the Search for the Ideal." *Annals of the Association of American Geographers* 62: 185–210.

WALLACH, BRET

1985   "The Return of the Prairie." *Landscape* 28(3): 1–5.

WEBB, LOREN

1983   "Millionaire keeps eye to the future." *The Daily Spectrum* (St. George, Utah), June 19.

WEBB, WALTER PRESCOTT
1936   *The Great Plains.* New York: Houghton-Mifflin.

WEST, N. E.
1983   *Temperate Deserts and Semi-Deserts.* Amsterdam: Elsevier Scientific.

WRITERS' PROGRAM
1940   *Arizona: A State Guide.* New York: Hastings House.

WUPATKI RUINS TRAIL
1982   Globe, Arizona: Southwest Parks and Monuments Association.

YOUNG, HERBERT
1972   *They Came to Jerome: The Billion Dollar Copper Camp.* Jerome, Arizona: Jerome Historical Society.

ZELINSKY, WILBUR
1973   *The Cultural Geography of the United States.* Englewood Cliffs: Prentice-Hall.

Index

ABOUT THE AUTHORS

THOMAS R. VALE has been a member of the faculty of the Department of Geography at the University of Wisconsin in Madison since 1973. He received his doctorate in geography from the University of California at Berkeley that same year. His early research documented the nature of controversy arising from natural resource issues in wilderness and parks. He is author of *Plants and People* (1982), an ecological evaluation of people-induced vegetation change, and is writing a book about protected wild nature as a resource.

GERALDINE R. VALE is a schoolteacher in the Madison Public Schools, where she has taught geography, English, and writing over the last fifteen years. She and her husband are coauthors of *u.s. 40 Today* (1983). Since 1983 they have been doing a comparative study of landscape change in Yosemite National Park, based on the photographs of early geologists.

Vale, Thomas R., 1943-
   Western images, western landscapes :
~~~~~~~ ~long U.S. 89 / Thomas R. Vale,
                                    :
                                    c1989.

DATE DUE

JUN 1 5 1992			
-2			
GAYLORD			PRINTED IN U.S.A.

and
pe--West
way 89.
. Vale,
s--West
--

89-5063